Midwest Morsels

MIDWEST MORSELS

Memorable Recipes and Reflections

By Laura Kurella

Edited By Anne Sutton

Hard Cover Edition ISBN: 978-0-9766303-9-5

Printed in the United States of America

\First Edition - November 6, 2022

Cover Photography and Design by Laura Kurella

Book Interior Photos (unless noted otherwise) by Laura Kurella

Book Interior Design by Laura Kurella

Please direct your inquiries to laurakurella@yahoo.com

Published by

Reality-Based Books

LTK

a division of

Laura Kurella, LLC

U.S.A

www.laurakurella.com

Special Thanks

To Whiting-Robertsdale Historical Society for photos and research assistance.

To Rick Grzywana for providing the Art's Drive-in photo from your collection.

To the Calumet Region establishments who continue to provide noteworthy meals.

To all my supporters. Thank you for your strength and encouragement. It fuels me!

To all my beloved siblings and friends who have contributed to this book.

To my family, especially my grandchildren, children, and husband. For letting me experiment on you, for your help, and for not minding (too much) that I am always wrong about how much time things take, like this project– whew! Your abiding patience with me makes me love you more every day!

This book was written entirely by me and is based solely on my own personal opinion.

All business information contained herein was sourced from personal experience or the internet. Should it contain errors, please notify me so that future editions may reflect updated information.

Photo by Richard Taylor: Laura in Boundary Waters at Quetico Provincial Park, Ontario Canada

May GOD and HIS Universal Positive Force <u>always</u> be with you!

i

thank

GOD

Midwest Morsels

Memorable Recipes and Reflections

By Laura Kurella

Edited by Anne Sutton

CONTENTS

The "Old Country"

According to my parents, I am a second generation American and the youngest of their seven children. However, my story doesn't begin there because our family home was so strongly influenced by our ancestors that I must start by going back to what our parents affectionately referred to as the "old country."

Learning through old documents and DNA that both sets of our grandparents were predominantly Eastern European, making me almost full-blooded (88%), official immigration documents uncovered during a family tree search by our eldest sister Jeanne revealed that our maternal grandfather was born in Hungary, in an area known as Roskoc and immigrated to America in 1906 aboard the Carpathia.

Through additional official documents, Jeanne was able to trace his family tree back to his grandparents, which revealed they were both born in Austria.

Jeanne also discovered that our paternal grandfather and his wife, Joanna, were both born in Wielki Bobrowiec, Hungary during the 1800s and that Grandpa came to America in 1913 aboard the Bremen. Jeanne was also able to successfully trace his family tree back to his grandmother, who was listed as being born in Austria.

By sheer coincidence (prior to my learning of this Austria connection), my dear friend Anne once teased me about my "MacGyver" like abilities, saying, "Who do you think you are, Hedy Lamarr?"

Not knowing who Ms. Lamarr was, Anne had to explain that Hedy was an Austrian-born film actress and inventor who used her "MacGyver" like abilities to help develop a radio guidance system for torpedoes that used spread spectrum and frequency hopping technology, which was so advanced at the time that it is still used to this day in Bluetooth, GPS, and Wi-Fi technology.

Sadly, Hedy never received any public recognition for her inventions during her lifetime, but was, at long last, inducted into the National Inventors Hall of Fame in 2014, exactly one hundred years after her birth and fourteen years after her death. God bless Hedy!

[FYI: There is an awesome (and sad) biography about Hedy Lamarr titled, "Bombshell: The Hedy Lamarr story"]

Learning about Hedy made me wonder if Dad's genius abilities came from having an Austrian bloodline, which passed some of his unique abilities, creativity, and a mind that never wants to quit passed down to us!

While none of us possess anything near the genius of Hedy, or Dad for that matter, we each did get a dusting that provides us all with some "MacGyver" like abilities. Thankfully, it is also being sprinkled down the bloodline onto our children and grandchildren too, who demonstrate the same "MacGyver" and kaizen-like strengths.

What's funny is that despite the official documents stating that the birthplace of both our grandfathers was indeed Hungary, my siblings and I have argued often about our nationality, especially since both our parents always maintained that we were "Slovak," a term used to define a region, much like "Midwest" is used in America today.

Our parents never mentioned the word "Hungarian" so long as either of them were alive. However, with legal census documents evidencing that out great-grandparents (on both sides) were born in Austria, which was definitely the Hungarian Empire at the time, and both grandparents also stating in legal documents that they too were born in Hungary, it became difficult for me to see my lineage as being anything but what was legally listed.

The way I see it, my family came from Slovak territories much in the same way we consider ourselves as coming from the Midwest today. Our ancestors considered themselves Hungarian much in the same way we consider ourselves as coming from Indiana, simply because we were all born there. However, we are not one or the other. We are, in fact, both.

Given that this area of the world had borders constantly shifting, especially Hungary, it should be no surprise that such an ambiguity came to exist. That being said, my dear cousin, Elizabeth Kurella (a world-renowned authority on lace) was fortunate to travel to Europe and visit the "old country" area where she spoke about lace, and then visited the very village that her father, my dad's brother, Istivan, was born.

While speaking at a lace congress (convention) in Halas, Hungary, Elizabeth told me, "When I mentioned that my ancestors were from the Tatra Mountains in Slovakia, my hosts brought me up short. 'You DO mean the Upper Hungarian Highlands, don't you?' A stiff reminder that when my great-grandparents were tending their orchards and sheep in the Tatra Mountains, it was part of the Austro-Hungarian Empire, and STILL is a part of that empire as far as those Hungarians in Halas are concerned!"

Elizabeth described the area as comparable in size to West Virginia, and having similar features with areas of small isolated villages hidden in the mountains and valleys.

With the borders of these nations dancing around, Elizabeth indicated that most of the bobbin lace styles made in the many regions of Slovakia were influenced by their "dance" partners too, which were the Czech Republic, Poland, Moravia, Germany, Russia, Sweden, and Italy.

While national borders were and still are doing a polka of sorts, the one thing that has never been overturned, or even shifted, is the rich culture and cuisine that still hails from these delightful ethnic resources to this day, thank God!

Mom relied heavily on "old county" recipes that she sourced from family, friends, and old Slovak cookbooks, which further evidence the blend of ethnicities by featuring Hungarian, Polish, Slovak, Russian, Romanian, and others side-by-side in cookbooks.
Many of Mom's own recipe iterations originated from these cookbooks, and a couple of her favorites were well-worn issues of the St. John's Rosary Society cookbook, a very old Slovak cook-book, and Betty Crocker, of course!

Using these cookbooks as guides, Mom's kitchen seemed to dance with her own unique rhythm. Rotating not only with the seasons, but also the holidays, and her own tastes, which is why whenever Easter came around we all knew we'd be peeling lots of potatoes for sausage!

As a child, I knew droby only as a sausage, and one that required a laborious sixty pounds of potatoes to be peeled. The potatoes were then ground with onion and pork and stuffed into beef casings before being boiled and stored (either in the fridge or freezer or both) for later use. Thanks to my cousin, Elizabeth Kurella, I've come to learn that this dish is an authentic recipe that is still served (and sold at markets) in our ancestor's native land.

Mom's "Old Country" Droby
(Eastern European Potato Sausage)
Yield: 40 servings
15 pounds Idaho russet potatoes
1 pound bone-in pork steak
1 pound uncured bacon
4 large sweet onions
1 tablespoon high quality salt
1 teaspoon freshly ground black pepper, or to taste
2 tablespoons dried marjoram
1 tablespoon dried mint
40 feet of beef or hog casings, well rinsed
Bring a large turkey roasting pan filled 3/4 of the way with water to a boil. Meanwhile, peel potatoes then cut into pieces that will fit in the grinder then place pieces in a container of very hot water, which will keep them white. In a large heavy skillet over high heat, fry pork steaks until crispy, about 5 minutes per side. Remove and set aside. Without cleaning the skillet, add bacon to the skillet and cook until crisp as well, about 4 minutes per side, then remove and set on top of pork steaks. Peel and slice onion then add it to the hot skillet with the drippings from the bacon and pork still in it. Cook onion over high heat, stirring, until the onion begins to caramelize, about 8 minutes. Remove pan from heat and set aside. Returning to pork, cut meat and fat away from bone, and into pieces that will fit into a grinder. Discard bone or reserve it for another use. Using a medium grinding blade, process onions, then bacon, then pork meat and fat, then finish by running drained potatoes through a grinder. Season with salt, pepper, marjoram, and mint, stirring to combine well.
Returning to skillet, over medium-high heat, scoop a tablespoon of the mixture into the hot pan and fry for about 4 minutes per side to sample, then adjust seasonings if necessary. Using the standard procedure for stuffing sausage, stuff mixture into prepared casings, leaving enough room on either end for expansion. Once the roasting pan of water comes to a boil, begin processing filled sausage links by pricking the sides of the sausage with a fork to help air escape and prevent ruptures. Boil sausage for 15 minutes per side to make sure potatoes are thoroughly cooked, which will prevent them from turning black. Once sausage is boiled, place on wire racks to drain and cool. Store sausage in the freezer until ready to use.
To cook, cut the desired amount of sausage and place in a hot skillet with butter to brown or slit the sausage open and place pats of butter on them and broil to desired doneness. Serve with butter, sour cream and/ or applesauce.
NOTE: Mixture can be cooked sans sausage casings, too. Simply add a few tablespoons of flour to the mixture before spreading it out in baking pans.
Bake at 350 degrees for 1 hour or until desired doneness (165 degrees) is reached.~

As Mom began to advance in years, she would on rare occasions make a tiny batch of droby then pour its contents into a brownie pan and bake it sans the casing. She didn't call the dish droby, but rather kugelis, and I am grateful that she took the time to write this iteration down for me on an old recipe card that I still have in my possession to this day.

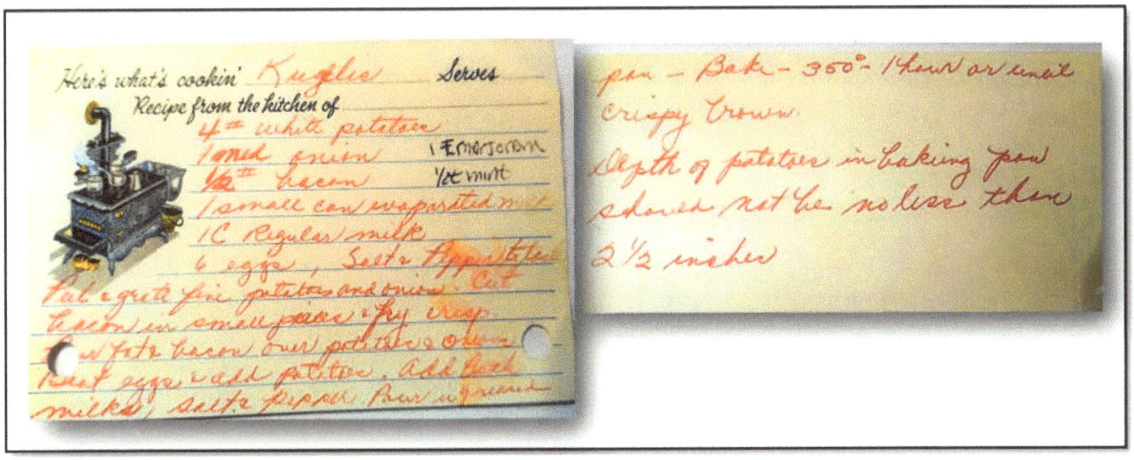

Never questioning it until cousin Elizabeth recently told me of her European experience, I looked up the term kugelis and found that it's used to describe a style of a dish, very similar to the American word casserole, and how the word itself is pronounced provides a clue as to where your ancestors hail from. If you say "COO-gu-l" your ancestors could be from Lithuania, northern Poland, or northern Russia (including Vilna, Minsk and Bialystock) and like it savory with meat. If your family calls it "KEE-gul" then your ancestors are likely from southern Poland and the Ukraine (including the cities of Chelm and Krakow), and your family prefers it sweet. Since my mother pronounced it "Coo-gu-la" and spelled it (according to her own handwriting) kugelis, one would have to assume that it is the Slovak version of this recipe, which leans in the savory-meaty direction that, I might add, makes it taste oh-so-good!

When I get a taste for droby, I put together a small pan's worth because it is close enough to "hit the spot" as they say, and my recipe for it does not make too much, or "grind" up an entire day!

Kurella's Easy Kugel

2 tablespoons avocado oil or butter
1 sweet yellow onion
1/2-pound uncured bacon
4 pounds Idaho Russet potatoes (remove 3 small potatoes from a 5# bag)
6 large eggs
2 teaspoons ground marjoram
1 teaspoon ground mint
1/2 teaspoon unrefined mineral sea salt
1 teaspoon fresh black pepper

Preheat the oven to 350 degrees. In a heavy skillet, fry bacon over medium-high heat until crisp. Meanwhile, peel and slice onion. Once bacon is cooked, remove from pan to a plate then add onion

slices to bacon grease and fry until they begin to caramelize, about 7 to 10 minutes.
In the bowl of a food processor, combine cooked bacon and onion and then process until they become particles. Peel potatoes then, cube and add to the processor. Pulse processor until potatoes are finely minced. Add eggs and spices then pulse processor just until well blended. Pour mixture into a greased 8 x 8 pan or casserole dish.
Place the pan in a preheated oven and bake for one hour or until crispy brown on top and center appears cooked. Remove from the oven and serve hot with butter, sour cream or applesauce, if desired. ~

Kugelis

Cirak

Cirak (Easter Cheese)
1-quart whole milk
1 teaspoon salt
1 to 3 dozen eggs, yolks punctured
1 cheesecloth bag
Spread four layers of cheesecloth out in a large colander, rinse with clean water then set aside, or use a cheesecloth bag. Set up a large double boiler over medium heat. Add milk and salt then, in a small clear glass cup or bowl, begin cracking eggs, a few at a time, being sure to fish out any shells and puncturing each yolk. Transfer punctured eggs into top pot of the double boiler and stir into the milk. Repeat with remaining eggs. Gently stir mixture, cooking until mixture resembles loose scrambled eggs. When water is visibly seen separating out the curds pour the loose curd mixture into cheesecloth. Once all egg mixture is transferred, tie the cheesecloth closed and hang/suspend for one hour, then set in the colander with heavy object on top of it to strain for 2 more hours. Afterwards, remove cheesecloth and place cheese in a sealed container and refrigerate until chilled before serving, about 4 hours. Delicious alone or paired with ham, especially on sandwiches. ~

Mom's Egg Bread

1 tablespoon butter (she used Land O' Lakes)
1 (12 ounce) can evaporated milk (Milnot)
1 cup warm water (not tap*)
2 teaspoons sugar (she used Domino Cane)
1 package (1/4 ounce) active dry yeast (Red Star)
6 cups all-purpose flour, divided use (Ceresota)
1 teaspoon salt
2 large egg yolks, beaten (farm-fresh)
Melted butter for basting finished loaf (optional)
*=Tap water may contain yeast-killing agents, which cause the recipe to fail. Use distilled or spring water.

In a small saucepan, melt butter then add evaporated milk and water. Stir then heat just to 100 degrees, no hotter or it will kill the yeast. Transfer milk mixture to the bowl of a mixer then add sugar, hand stirring to help dissolve, then sprinkle in yeast.

With a paddle attachment, and mixer set to lowest speed, slowly adding just one cup of flour and salt.

Once blended in, add egg yolks. Beat on medium speed for 5 minutes then reduce speed to lowest setting and slowly add more flour until a soft dough forms.

Remove dough from the mixer bowl and turn out onto a surface that is floured with remaining flour. Knead by hand until remaining flour is absorbed into dough and texture becomes smooth and elastic, about 5 minutes' worth of kneading should do. Place in a greased bowl, turning once to grease top. Cover loosely with a towel and let rise in a warm place until doubled, about 2 hours.

Remove dough from bowl, turning out onto a barely floured surface. Divide dough in half, setting one piece aside, covered.

Working with one piece at a time, roll dough out and then, using a knife, cut into 3 lengthy pieces. Shape each piece into a 12-inch rope then braid the three pieces together, pinching ends to seal. Scoop up braid and place into a buttered 6 x 10 (or similar) loaf pan, tucking ends under as you set in place. Set the loaf on top of the stove (or warm area), cover with a warm towel then repeat the same steps with the remaining dough.

Let loaves rise in a warm spot until doubled, about 30 minutes, then begin to preheat the oven to 375 degrees, so bread has a little more time for final rise.

Place in the oven and bake for 30 minutes then rotate pans, both switching sides and rotating loaves so the end pointing to the back of the oven is now facing front, then continue to bake another 30 minutes. Cover with foil during the last 15 minutes of baking.

Remove from pan to a wire rack to cool slightly, then brush the tops of the loaves with melted butter, (if desired). ~

Eastern European Potica (Nut roll bread)

Yield: 12 servings

DOUGH

1 teaspoon active dry yeast
3/4 cup milk
2 tablespoons white sugar
3 egg yolks
1 teaspoon unrefined mineral sea salt
1/2 cup very soft butter
2 1/2 cups all-purpose flour

FILLING

1/2 cup melted butter
6 ounces honey
1 cup raisins (optional)
3/4- pound ground walnuts
ground cinnamon, for dusting

In the bowl of a stand mixer fitted with the paddle attachment place yeast, milk, sugar, egg yolks, salt, and very soft butter. Blend until ingredients are mixed well. Replace paddle attachment with dough hook and add the flour. Run the mixer at medium speed for 10 minutes or until the dough has good gluten development. Dust with flour, cover the bowl with a clean dish towel, and let rise for 2 hours.

Place risen dough on a floured board and roll out to one thin rectangle. Baste dough with melted butter, then drizzle with honey, sprinkle with raisins, if using, then sprinkle/spread the ground walnuts. Dust generously with cinnamon then roll up like a jelly roll. Grease or spray a 2-pound loaf pan, coil rolled-up log of dough into a "U" shape on the bottom of the pan, then double back and coil a second U shape on the pan. Place on stovetop or warm area, cover with greased or sprayed plastic wrap, and let rise for one hour.

Preheat the oven to 350 degrees. Place the pan in the oven and let it bake for 30 minutes then rotate the pan and cover the top of the loaf with foil if it starts to get too brown. Bake another 30 minutes or until a tester inserted in the center of the loaf comes out clean, not sticky, and the internal temperature reads at least 185 degrees. Cool in pan for 20 minutes before turning out onto a cooling rack. ~

With the stroke of a fingertip or the click of a mouse anyone can discover the origin and nationality of a recipe today. For example, one recipe Mom would make for us often (that we still adore) is Chicken Paprikash, a dish with firm, deep roots in Hungary.
Being very specific about what ingredients she'd use, Mom was very persnickety about the paprika. Insisting on a fresh can of Budapest's Finest Sweet Hungarian Paprika, Mom said to use only it because, as she put it, "It's simply the best there is!"

Mom always began this recipe with lots of chopped sweet onion that she'd caramelize in the bottom of her big, heavy-bottomed pressure cooker. Her trick for getting it to taste its best was to sear the chicken over the highest heat possible after she coated each piece very heavily with what can only be described as a red blanket of paprika. Once all the chicken was seared well, she would add water and bouillon then pressure cook it until the meat fell off the bones. She'd finish this dish by removing the chicken to cool slightly then skin and debone it. Then she'd take the remaining liquid and pour it into a tall glass so she could skim the fat off the top and return it to the skillet to make what she called "zapraska," which I discovered is Russian for "roux." (FYI: in Slovak it's called "zaprazhit") To the roux she'd add a rich and rewarding amount of sour cream; and to make it extra amazing, she always made fresh egg dumplings!

When discussing the making of this cookbook, sister Jeanne told me to make sure Mom's Chicken Paprikash recipe got in- Done!

Mom's "Old Country" Chicken Paprikash (adapted for 6 servings)

2 tablespoons butter (add more as needed)
2 medium sweet onions, chopped
2 chicken legs with thighs
2 chicken breasts, whole
1 tablespoon Hungarian sweet paprika
4 cups water
5 chicken bouillon cubes
1/4 cup all-purpose flour
1-pint sour cream

DUMPLINGS
1 gallon water
2 cups all-purpose flour
1 teaspoon salt
2 large eggs
3/4 cup water

In a large Dutch oven over medium heat, melt butter. Sprinkle chicken generously with paprika then add to hot pan in uncrowded batches, searing chicken on all sides, about 7-10 minutes. Remove to a platter or baking pan. Once all chicken has been seared, add chopped onion to drippings from the chicken in the Dutch oven and cook over medium-high heat until onions begin to caramelize, about 5 minutes. Return chicken to pan, add water and bouillon cubes. Bring to a boil, then reduce heat to simmer, cover and cook over low heat for 30 minutes. Meanwhile, make dumplings. Start by placing 1 gallon water in a large pot and bring to a boil over high heat. While water is heating, combine flour, salt, and baking powder in a medium bowl. In another bowl or cup, whisk eggs with water and slowly stir into flour mixture until dough is wet, but is firm and holds together well. Add more water if the dough is too stiff. Once water is boiling, place about a cup of the dumpling dough on a flat-rimmed plate, then dip a teaspoon (utensil, not measure) into the boiling water to heat it. Use the hot teaspoon to scrape a scant spoonful of the dumpling dough off the plate into the boiling water, being sure to dip the spoon into the boiling water each time you drop a dumpling in to keep the spoon hot. This will help keep the dumpling dough from sticking to the spoon. Once the dumplings are all in the boiling water, reduce heat to low, cover the pot and let simmer for 10 to 12 minutes, then drain and set aside.

When chicken is finished braising, remove pieces from the Dutch oven to another dish or pan to cool slightly, discarding any errant skin and bones. Strain the liquid from the pan into a clear glass vessel. Let liquid settle so that fat has the chance to float to top. Meanwhile, sort through the solids strained out, removing any undesirable skin, gristle, or bones, then set aside. [Alternately, discard strained solids or reserve for a different use.] Return to liquid, skim all the fat off, and return it to the un-clean Dutch oven. Move remaining liquid to the cup of a blender. Add the picked clean onion solids, if using, and puree until smooth then set next to the stove. To the fat in the pan, add 1/4 cup flour and place over medium heat, stirring constantly, to create the "zapraska" (roux). Once the zapraska has bubbled for about 3 minutes, and begun to turn brown, slowly begin adding the prepared liquid, stirring constantly, whisk the strained liquid into the zapraska and cook until thickened. Reduce heat to low and cover. In a heatproof container microwave sour cream until warm then whisk into zapraska. Add dumplings, stir to break apart. Skin and debone chicken then fold gently in and serve immediately.~

Though many are intimidated by dumplings, it's just a loose noodle dough scraped off a plate into boiling water. The trick is to heat the spoon in the boiling water both before use and after every scoop of dough, which is why I continually submerge my spoon into the boiling water with each scoop, before returning it to the plate to scrape more dough into the pot. To make tiny dumplings, simply scoop less, or switch out the spoon for a butter knife.

As a child, Mom welcomed me into her kitchen as a mini sous chef, entrusting me with the mindful duty of carefully peeling away the outer, paper-thin, brown skin on sweet yellow onions that she seemed to need every time she cooked.

I didn't realize until well into adulthood that everyone else didn't cook at all like Mom, adding onions to the skillet before anything. This led me to believe that whenever I happen to see an errant onion skin in someone's kitchen is quite likely an Eastern European!

One of my favorite recipes that Mom once told me was from the "old country" I recall her making especially during Lent, which is a special time that Roman Catholics observe during the forty days that lead up to Easter to help with spiritual renewal and reflection.

As kids we were not allowed to laugh too much or eat too much, especially meat, which is why her amazing meatless, and loaded with sweet onion potato pancakes would be served.

To me, Mom's potato pancakes were not what I considered a sacrifice. They imparted such an awesome aroma that it would hit you the moment you walked in the door. The incredible oniony aroma dragged me by my nose straight into her kitchen where I would always beg for more.

I liked them so much, in fact, that I used to beg Mom to make them more often than Lent,

but she wouldn't. As a result, once I got my own kitchen, I would indulge in them more often and I even developed a way to make the fabulous ones that Chicago delis are known to sell. The kind that tastes like a cross between a potato pancake and a fritter. That recipe should come with a warning to indulge responsibly because it is easy to overeat those. So good!

Mom's Perfect Potato Pancakes

Yield: 4 servings

1/4 cup milk

2 large russet potatoes, peeled and chunked

1 medium sweet onion, quartered

2 eggs

3 tablespoons all-purpose flour

1 pinch baking powder

Place all ingredients in a blender, in the order given, then blend, pulsing well until pureed. Pour, by tablespoon, onto a hot griddle that has been greased with vegetable shortening. Flip cakes when edges begin to brown. Salt and pepper, to taste. Great served with sour cream or applesauce ~

Old Chicago Deli-style Potato Pancakes

Yield: 6 servings

5 medium white (Idaho) russet potatoes, peeled

1 large yellow sweet onion

2 beaten eggs

2 tablespoons all-purpose flour

Using a grinder or hand-grater, grind the onions then grind the potatoes, mixing into the onion as you grind to prevent the potatoes from turning black.

Line a colander with cheesecloth or a loosely woven linen towel then transfer potato/onion mixture into it. Allow the mixture to sit and drain for 10 minutes then press slightly to release more liquid, discarding all the fluids that drain away. Transfer drained potato/onion mixture to a bowl and add remaining ingredients, stirring well. If the batter is not thick enough, add a bit more flour. Add a half-inch of shortening to a deep skillet. When the shortening is hot, spoon the batter into the shortening by 1/2 cup ladlesful. Brown on both sides, turning only once. Salt and pepper, to taste. ~

Cabbage played a big role in lots of the "old country" dishes and Mom said it was because it provided lots of nutrition, health, fiber, and fuel for little money. Plus, cabbage is a good "keeper" so people were able to grow lots of it, store it in their cellars and survive the harsh winter.

This is also the reason she gave for there being white russet potatoes in lots of the recipes as well, adding that combining potatoes and cabbage kept lots of poor people from dying from starvation, especially during the Great Depression.

Mom also made the comment once that she thought God planned the vegetables this way so that all souls could afford to eat delicious meals.

To me there is something unique that potatoes bring to a dish and you notice their absence when removed. Such is the case when making haluski and substituting plain or egg noodles for the potato dumplings. It does not taste the same, so if you don't have the time to make the dumplings, wait until you do.

The Whiting-Robertsdale area was loaded with small, "Mom and Pop" corner markets and many of the corners in the area still have the storefronts intact, even though they have been converted to residential housing or other forms of business.

Mom's "Old Country" Haluski

Yield: 6 servings

1 head of cabbage, finely hand-chopped
1 large, sweet onion, finely hand-chopped
1 stick butter
2 large russet (Idaho) potatoes, peeled
1 egg
3 cups all-purpose flour

In a Dutch oven, combine chopped cabbage, onion, butter, and salt to taste, about 1 teaspoon. Simmer on low heat until mixture is evenly browned, about 1.25 hours. Meanwhile, bring a large pot of water to a boil over high heat. In a medium bowl, blend eggs with salt to taste, about a teaspoon, then grate potato into them, stirring as you grate to prevent potatoes from darkening. Add flour and stir gently to blend well. Dough should be slightly loose, but not thin, so add more flour if the potato is adding more moisture. Once water comes to a full rolling boil, place dumpling dough on a plate then, using a teaspoon, dip spoon into boiling water to get hot then use the hot spoon to scrape small scoops of dough into the boiling water, dipping spoon each time into boiling water to help release dough and to keep spoon hot. Repeat until all dough is in the boiling water. Bring the pot to a boil then reduce to a simmer and cook for 15 minutes to make sure the potato is cooked through. Otherwise, dumplings will turn black. Once dumplings are finished cooking, strain with a colander and set aside until cabbage and onion are finished cooking. When the cabbage mixture has finished cooking, add dumplings to the pan, stir to blend in dumplings well, then serve.~

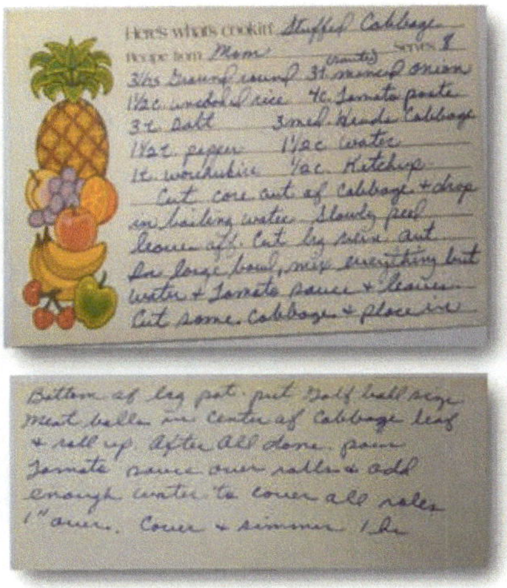

Here's what's cookin' Stuffed Cabbage
Recipe from Mom Serves 8
3lbs Ground round 3T. minced onion
1 1/2c uncooked rice 4c. Tomato paste
3t. Salt 3 med. heads Cabbage
1 1/2t. pepper 1 1/2c water
1t. worchestire 1/2c. Ketchup
Cut core out of Cabbage + drop in boiling water. Slowly peel leaves off. Cut big veins out. In large bowl, mix everything but water + Tomato sauce + leaves. Cut some Cabbage + place in Bottom of big pot. put Golf ball size Meat balls in center of Cabbage leaf + roll up. After All done, pour Tomato sauce over rolls + add enough water to cover all roles 1" over. Cover + simmer 1 hr

Mom's Stuffed Cabbage aka Halupki was always a delight to eat, but I didn't like the cabbage on the rolls, so she always made some porcupine balls, too!

Pan Roasted Porcupine Balls

Yield: 8 servings
3/4 cup uncooked long grain rice
1 1/2 pounds ground red meat, your choice
3/4 cup chicken broth or stock, low sodium
1 teaspoon celery flakes
1 teaspoon black pepper
1 teaspoon garlic powder
30 ounces tomato sauce
2 cups water
1/4 cup brown sugar
1 tablespoon Worcestershire sauce

Preheat the oven to 350 degrees. In a hot dry skillet over high heat, toast dry rice for a few minutes by stirring constantly then place rice in a 2-cup bowl and cover with the hottest tap water. Let rice rest like this for 10 minutes. Meanwhile, gather and measure out all the rest of the ingredients you will need. Once time has elapsed, place rice in a screen strainer and drain off liquid. In a mixing bowl (hand or stand), combine meat, rinsed rice, broth, celery flakes, pepper, and garlic powder, and mix (by hand or with mixer) until well combined. Remove from the mixer and form into golf balls or larger size meatballs. Place in a single layer into a greased 3-quart sized casserole dish or roasting pan. In another bowl, combine tomato sauce, 2 cups water, brown sugar, and Worcestershire sauce, blending well, then pour over top of the balls. Cover the pan tightly with foil and bake for one hour 15 minutes.~

Sister Diane Method: In a crock pot, heat sauce ingredients to boiling then add balls, gently covering with sauce. Cover and cook on "high" for 4 hours.

As I got older, I learned that Mom was taking this exact recipe and switching out the cabbage for bell peppers. This got me to thinking that they might benefit from a little flavor elevation through additional ingredients, which led me to develop my own version of what was clearly rooted in "old country" cuisine.

Spectacular Stuffed Peppers

Yield: 6 servings

6 fresh bell peppers

1 pound ground beef

1/2 cup Jasmine rice

1 small onion, minced

1 cup chicken broth

2 tablespoons dark brown sugar

1 tablespoon soy sauce

1 tablespoon oyster sauce

1 tablespoon ground ginger

2 cloves garlic, minced

1 teaspoon coarsely ground pepper

1/4 cup fresh orange juice

15 ounce can tomato sauce

Preheat oven to 350 degrees. Slice off the stem end of peppers and reserve for later. Remove the seeds and membranes from the peppers and rinse peppers inside and out. Place peppers face up in a baking dish just large enough to accommodate all peppers. In mixer, with paddle attachment, combine meat, rice, onion, brown sugar, soy sauce, garlic, oyster sauce, pepper ginger, orange juice, and 1 cup chicken broth; stir until well combined. Fill each pepper with the beef mixture. Pour tomato sauce evenly over the peppers and cover the baking dish tightly. Bake for 2 hours then serve. Dish freezes well.~

Mom's From Scratch Barbecue Sauce

2 tablespoons butter
1 medium onion, diced
1/4 cup diced celery
1 cup water
1 cup ketchup
3 tablespoons brown sugar
3 tablespoons lemon juice
3 tablespoons Worchester sauce
3 tablespoons distilled white vinegar

In a deep, heavy skillet, melt butter. Add diced onion and celery and brown well, then add water, ketchup, brown sugar, lemon juice, Worchester sauce, and vinegar. Bring to a boil and simmer for 30 minutes, stirring occasionally.

NOTE: To help this sauce "cling" to ribs or chicken, in a small cup, liquefy 1 tablespoon of cornstarch in 2 tablespoons of cold water then whisk it into the sauce at the end of the simmering time. Be sure to bring sauce up to a good boil before removing from heat. Yield: 8 servings ~

Mom's Amazing Ribs
Yield: 8 servings
6 pounds ribs
2 tablespoons sweet Hungarian paprika (Mom used Budapest's Finest)
2 tablespoons garlic powder (Mom used light blue-capped Lawry's)
2 tablespoons seasoned tenderizer (Mom used yellow-capped Adolph's)
Preheat broiler. Combine seasonings then generously sprinkle over ribs. Broil ribs on both sides until well browned. Preheat oven to 325 degrees. Cut ribs into portion-size pieces then place into a large roasting pan, coating each piece with a generous amount of barbecue sauce. Cover roasting pan and bake for 1hour, basting ribs occasionally. Then remove roaster from oven, baste ribs well, rotate pan and return to oven to roast, uncovered for the final hour, basting occasionally. ~

Mom's Special Sloppy Joes
Yield: 8 servings
2 tablespoons butter
3 stalks celery, chopped
1 sweet onion, chopped
2 pounds ground round
1 cup ketchup
3/4 cup water
3 tablespoons brown sugar
3 tablespoons lemon juice
3 tablespoons Worchester sauce
3 tablespoons distilled white vinegar
In a large skillet, brown onion, and celery in butter. Add meat and cook until crumbled and brown. Stir in remaining ingredients, simmer covered for 1 hour, stirring occasionally. ~

I love the earthy-musky-sweet-woodsy scent of those lovely umber-hued autumn leaves. Inextricably linked to memories of jumping feet first into a huge piles of them, this childhood ritual was part tradition and part rite of passage that was always guaranteed to make our cheeks blush a chilly, rosy red!

It was easy to while away an entire afternoon with a rake and some leaves and often the only thing able to tear us away would be the amazing autumnal-spiced aroma that would waft from Mom's kitchen.

Filling the air with earthy-spicy plumes of cinnamon, clove and nutmeg, Mom would mingle the spices with crisp fall fruit and butter then swaddle it in uncountable, butter-flaky layers of super-thin, hand-stretched strudel dough that combined to create a treat so delightful that the mere act of recalling it causes me to drool!

Strudel has a long and interesting history and while many thought it was German in origin, research has shown that this pastry stretches back to the 17th century Austria, which is evidenced in a handwritten recipe for milk strudel dated 1696 that is well-preserved in the Vienna Town Hall Library.

Likely the result of cultures collaborating over time, this pastry has close variations in Turkish baklava, Greek spanakopita, and more.

While creating a true strudel completely from scratch does require getting down your own technique for stretching this very elastic dough, today many skip this step and simply buy sheets of phyllo from the freezer section at the store. Granted, it will not taste near as amazing as it does if you take the time to make it completely from scratch, but it does get you a freshly-baked strudel in a flash!

Today's strudel can have just about anything you want stuffed into it from cream cheese and berries to potatoes or even spinach and garlic like the Greek do. For me, it wouldn't be autumn without making a strudel with fresh-picked apples or ricotta cheese, like Mom used to.

Mom had to take over the dining room in order to have a large enough space to stretch out the dough for her strudel. I remember Dad taking these photos with his newest Polaroid which, according to the date written on them, occurred on June 12, 1972.

Austrian (Viennese) Apple Strudel

Yield: 8-10 servings

DOUGH

1/3 cup lukewarm water

1 tablespoon plus 1/2 teaspoon vegetable oil

1/2 teaspoon vinegar

1/8 teaspoon unrefined mineral sea salt

1 cup all-purpose flour

1/2 teaspoon vegetable oil, for brushing dough

flour for dusting

FILLING

3 tablespoons unsalted butter

2/3 cup fine bread crumbs

5 tablespoons cane sugar

1/2 teaspoon ground cinnamon

3 tablespoons rum or lukewarm water

1/4 cup raisins

2 pounds sweet-tart apples* (like MacIntosh)

1 tablespoon lemon juice

2 tablespoons melted butter, for brushing the dough (divided use)

confectioner's sugar for dusting (optional)

whipped cream for serving (optional)

To make dough, in a large hand bowl, or stand mixer bowl, combine lukewarm water, oil, vinegar and salt.

Stir in about half the flour with a spoon until well combined, then gradually add the remaining flour until it comes together and you can work it with your hands. Knead dough until smooth, about 10 minutes, either in the bowl with a mixer or on a working surface.

The dough should be moist but not sticky. If it is too sticky to knead, add a little more flour (you shouldn't need more than 1 or 2 additional tablespoons). Slam the dough onto the work surface a few times to enhance gluten development, yielding a very elastic dough. Shape the dough into a smooth ball. Brush a large, clean bowl with oil then place the dough into the bowl, and brush/ spray it with oil. Cover the bowl with a lid or plastic wrap and let it sit for 1 hour at room temperature. Meanwhile, start to make the filling.

In a small saucepan over medium heat, melt butter then add the breadcrumbs. Toast them, stirring constantly, until they are golden. Remove from heat and let cool. In a small bowl, combine sugar with cinnamon then add it to the buttered breadcrumbs, stirring well. Set aside. In a 1-cup glass measure or similar, measure rum (traditional) or lukewarm water then add raisins. Let soak until they soften, about 30 minutes.

Peel, quarter, and core apples then slice every quarter into 1/8 to 1/4 inch thick slices. Move sliced apples into a bowl then sprinkle with lemon juice to prevent apples from getting brown. Add the soaked raisins, discarding any remaining liquid in them, and mix well. Preheat the oven to 375 degrees.

Using a rolling pin on a large, clean, and lightly floured surface, roll out dough. Lightly flour the surface and the dough every now and then while rolling to prevent sticking. When the dough gets about 13-15 inches in diameter, pick it up then use the back of your hands, particularly your knuckles, to stretch it and straighten the dough like you would a pizza. When dough gets bigger and thinner, and difficult to handle, put it down on a lightly floured tablecloth (or sheet), straighten out the wrinkles in both the tablecloth and the dough. Continue stretching the dough on the tablecloth using your hands. Gently stretch the dough to a paper-thin thickness from the inside to the outside, working your way around the sheet of dough. Stretch it until it starts to look translucent.

You should be able to read through it. Your sheet of dough should be stretched into a rectangular shape, with the shorter edge fitting the baking sheet lengthwise. Thick edges should be cut off. Brush half the dough with half the melted butter. Spread the breadcrumb-mixture over the other half of the dough and pat down evenly. One side is brushed with butter now, the other side is covered with breadcrumbs. Leave 1 to 1 1/2 inch to the edge.

Spread the apples over the breadcrumbs. Fold in the side-ends of the dough. Using the tablecloth, roll the dough, starting at the apple-topped end all the way. Then gently roll the strudel onto a sheet of parchment paper with the seam-side down. Move strudel onto a baking pan then brush the top of it with remaining melted butter. Use a knife to cut vent slits on top, if desired. Place the pan on the middle rack of the preheated oven and bake it until crispy and golden brown, about 45 minutes. Remove from oven, let cool slightly, cut it into pieces, then serve dusted with confectioner's sugar, if desired.

NOTE: Dough can be made ahead and kept refrigerated for up to two (2) days. Return dough to room temperature before using.~

Easy Apple Strudel
1/3 cup raisins
2 tablespoons water
1 teaspoon pure almond extract
3 cups coarsely chopped, peeled apples, tossed with 2 tablespoons lemon juice
1/3 cup plus 2 teaspoons sugar, divided use
3 tablespoons all-purpose flour
1/4 teaspoon ground cinnamon
2 tablespoons butter, melted
2 tablespoons light oil
8 sheets phyllo dough (1/4 of the package)

Preheat oven to 350 degrees. Microwave raisins with water on high for 1-1/2 minutes, add almond extract, stir, rest for 5 minutes then discard liquid. In a large bowl, combine raisins, apples, 1/3 cup sugar, flour, and cinnamon. Mix well then set aside. In a small bowl, combine melted butter and oil. Place one sheet of phyllo dough on a work surface covered in parchment paper larger than the sheet. Brush/sprinkle lightly with butter mixture. Repeat 7 times then spread apple mixture over top to within 2 inches of one of the long sides, leaving about an inch on both short sides. Fold the short side edges over filling, then carefully roll up jelly-roll style, using parchment, starting from the side without the 2-inch border. Transfer roll to a baking sheet. Brush with remaining butter mixture and sprinkle with remaining 2 teaspoons of sugar. With a sharp knife, cut diagonal vent slits in top of strudel then bake until golden brown, about 35-45 minutes. Cool on a wire rack then, if desired, dust with powdered sugar before serving.

Baking wasn't Mom's work, it was her SUPER POWER!

It enabled her to make a positive difference in the lives of others, bring joy, and leave lasting memories that people still savor to this day, GOD bless her!

Here, at age 79, Mom was still rolling out her famous rosky (and nut rolls, too).

Mom didn't rest until she got into her 80s.
I am grateful she did get to enjoy her remaining years free of baking before leaving us at age 88.

Mom's tools of the trade were all custom made to fit her hand by Dad. Industrial grade, they included a special blunt-edged knife for spreading filling on nut rolls, a hand-hewn maple mixing spoon used for making the nut filling, and a custom nickel stainless rosky dough cutter that is still super sharp and quick as a whip!

Pastry-making is a tradition that is welded into Eastern European ancestry and one that I consider myself blessed to have. After all, not everyone got to wake up throughout childhood to fresh and sweet homemade pastry!

Growing up in the Calumet Region had the advantage of being a veritable melting pot of ethnicities, Polish, Irish, Slovak, Hungarian, Romanian, Lithuanian, German, and others who immigrated there for work bearing their former country's most prized and treasured of recipes! The influx of diversity caused not only a population explosion, but a gastric explosion as well. Many delicious recipes were everywhere, and the best of the best were so cherished they were, thanks be to GOD, written and handed down, which is how Mom learned to make rosky.

A pastry that goes by several names and called anything from rosky to nut horns to kolacky and more, depending upon nationality. The big take away is that they are so good that every ethnicity made sure to have their own version of it.

For those not familiar, rosky are a petite roll-like pastry that is folded in various ways to enclose the filling in its core. The most common fillings are prune, poppyseed, apricot, apple, blueberry, raspberry, or nut, unless you are our cousin Elizabeth, that is!

From what I was told by Mom, this pastry came into being because prior to food wraps the fruit on open-faced buns would get all over a working man's lunch bucket. Wives decided to devise a method of cooking the fruit down into a paste then folding it into a pastry, so it wouldn't mess up any lunch buckets!

Though debated as to whether the root recipe was of Hungarian, Slovak or Polish descent (Mom said she thought her recipe was Polish), the one thing that has never been disputed is its fabulous taste. In fact, it's so adored by the people of Montgomery, Minnesota that they have been holding an annual festival to honor the Czech version, kolacky, since 1929!

[FYI: Learn more about this fest at: montgomerymn.org.]

Mom was proud of this little pastry and once even told me a story about how she somehow managed to get some of them (and a nut roll) to John Wayne! She was so thrilled to hear that Mr. Wayne proclaimed, "These sure taste dandy!"

In her lifetime, Mom did dole out lots of these petite pastries and she did the same with her recipe for them too, but anyone who ever tried making them usually said they never tasted like hers. Perhaps that was because her secret ingredient was her own tender loving care!

Rolling them into tiny rolls, Mom preferred this style over others because it enabled her to put more filling into the pastry, and prevent it from leaking out all over the pan. She also noted that in later years the addition of high fructose corn syrup (to the canned fruit fillings available at the store) was causing the filling to melt the pastry dough, so she had to use less filling to keep the pastry crisp. I avoid these issues by simply turning fresh apricots, peaches and plums (in the summer) into fillings I store in freezer bags (in freezer) for winter use.

Mom's Rosky

1/2 cup butter
1/2 cup margarine
8 ounces cream cheese
2 1/2 cups flour
1 pound apricot filling
Powdered sugar for dusting

In the bowl of a mixer, combine butter, margarine, and cream cheese. Cream at high speed for 5 minutes then reduce mixer speed to low and slowly add in flour until a dough forms that cleans the side of mixing bowl. Remove from mixer, roll dough out in a baton then wrap in plastic wrap and place in the refrigerator. Chill completely, about 5 hours, or overnight.

When you are ready to make the pastries, preheat oven to 375 degrees and remove dough from refrigerator. Cut dough into 3 equal size pieces.

On a rolling board sprinkled with cane sugar, using a rolling pin, roll out one piece of the dough until it is 1/8-inch thick. Using a cookie wheel, pizza wheel, a knife, or a cookie cutter, cut dough into 2-inch circles or squares. With a dull end butter knife, dab 1/2 teaspoon of filling onto the center of each cookie then fold or roll as desired. Place on a greased aluminum baking sheet and bake for 10 to 12 minutes or until lightly crispy and brown. Cool slightly on rack before removing from pan. Cool pastry completely then dust lightly with powdered sugar before serving, if desired.

NOTE: Mom used the same nut filling for the rosky as she did her nut roll. Yield: 60 pastries ~

Cousin Elizabeth Kurella's Family Roshky

Yield: About 8 dozen cookies

3-1/2 cups all-purpose flour, divided use
juice of 1 lemon
3 egg yolks, beaten
3/4 cup water
1 pound butter

In a mixing bowl fitted with a paddle attachment, combine 1 1/2 cups of flour with the egg yolks, lemon juice and water. Mix on medium speed for 20 minutes. Remove from mixing bowl and turn out onto a well-floured surface. Roll the dough out until it reaches a 1/4-inch thickness then set aside and cover. To mixing bowl, add remaining 2 cups of flour and butter. Mix until well-blended and smooth. Using a knife, spread butter/flour mixture evenly over rolled out sheet of dough, then fold dough over on itself in half and then fold over on itself in half again. Wrap in waxed paper and refrigerate for two hours. Remove from refrigerator and roll out to original 1/4-inch thickness and fold as before again. Repeat this rolling and refrigerating process until you have done it 4 times. Once folding process is complete, place dough on a well-floured surface and divide into 3 even pieces.

Preheat oven to 375 degrees. Roll dough out one piece at a time, to desired thickness then cut into 2-inch squares. Place desired fillings (savory or sweet) on the corner of each square then roll to the other corner, pressing to seal. Place on an ungreased cookie sheet and bake for 20 minutes or until desired browning occurs.~

Cousin Elizabeth dazzled me by rolling out her family's version of roshky on an old desktop from St. John's that her father, Uncle Steve, re-purposed into a lovely rolling board. Elizabeth then delighted me by serving her puff pastry-like treat, which she further elevated with fancy fillings of savory and sweet treats. Elizabeth also gifted me a very old St. John's desktop so that I could try my hand at sanding down, too!

Aunt Gen's Potato Roll Recipe : She made these every Thanksgiving and Christmas and they were delicious. Grandpa loved them.

1 cup raw diced potatoes
2 cups water
1/2 cake yeast
4cups flour

1 1/2 teaspoons salt
1 tablespoon sugar
3 tablespoons fat (probably crisco)

Boil potatoes in water until tender. Drain and put through a sieve. Save 1 cup potato water, if necessary add more water to make 1 cup of liquid. Sift 3 1/2 cups flour with salt and sugar. Rub in fat with finger tips. Add disolved yeast and potatoes. Knead until it springs back when pressed with fingers. Add remaining half cup of flour, if needed. Place in greased bowl, brush with fat and cover. Let rise until doubled in bulk. Pinch off small pieces and shape lightly into round balls. Place 3 balls together in greased muffin tins, cover and let rise until double in bulk. Bake for about 25 minutes in moderately hot oven. 350 to 400 degrees. Serve hot.

I learned from cousin Susan that Aunt Genevieve (aka Aunt Gen) had an "old Country" recipe that she used on special occasions, such as Thanksgiving. Susan was kind enough to send it my way many years ago (God bless you!), so I am blessed to share it with you.

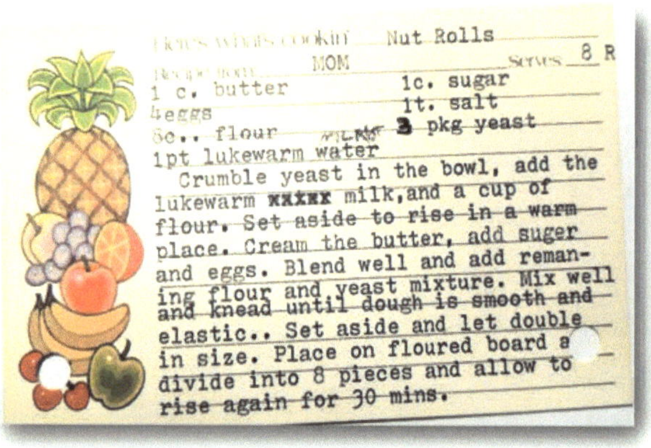

Nut Rolls
MOM Serves 8 R
1 c. butter
4eggs
8c.. flour
1pt lukewarm water
1c. sugar
1t. salt
3 pkg yeast

Crumble yeast in the bowl, add the lukewarm xxxxx milk,and a cup of flour. Set aside to rise in a warm place. Cream the butter, add suger and eggs. Blend well and add remaning flour and yeast mixture. Mix well and knead until dough is smooth and elastic.. Set aside and let double in size. Place on floured board a divide into 8 pieces and allow to rise again for 30 mins.

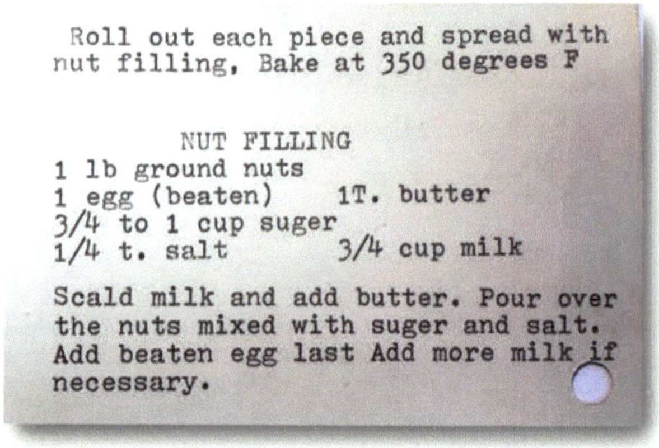

Roll out each piece and spread with nut filling, Bake at 350 degrees F

NUT FILLING
1 lb ground nuts
1 egg (beaten) 1T. butter
3/4 to 1 cup suger
1/4 t. salt 3/4 cup milk

Scald milk and add butter. Pour over the nuts mixed with suger and salt. Add beaten egg last Add more milk if necessary.

If I had to choose, I would have to say that Mom was perhaps best known for her nut roll, and I think it was because she poured her heart and soul into making them.

Her meticulous nature was automatic, not forced. She was a perfectionist when it came to baking, and to a degree that I have never seen in anyone outside of my own family.

In all honesty, Mom was among the elite few in our area whose name was synonymous with the best nut rolls you could find. It was an honor that humbled her and one she did not take lightly.

Our maternal great grandparents, Anna (Lesko) and Jan in Austria with four of their six children. Their son Michael (not pictured) would grow up, marry, and become Mom's dad.

When Whiting 'Fix-it' Needs Something Mechanical He Gets Busy and Makes It

(Left) Putting a few holes in a piece of brass tubing is done by Albert Kurella with his hand operated drill press.

Robertsdale Men Leave for Active Service

Making the news at age 19, in July of 1942, Dad had the local spotlight thrust upon him for being known as the local mechanical genius. Many predicted he was headed for a career to likely parallel that of Edison or the Wright Brothers. Ironically, just a few months later, Dad would make the newspaper again, this time in a notice of those shipping out for active duty in the war.

Our father, or "Dad" or "Daddy" as we called him, was considered nothing less than a genius by anyone that knew him, and it was a moniker that got attached to him well before he even reached adulthood, too.

I was in awe of Dad's brilliance to the point that I tried to make myself a literal sponge in his presence. I wanted to soak up everything he dispensed because there was just so much wisdom and knowledge constantly dripping from his tongue. He wasn't just a dad, he was my idol, and though he was flawed as all humans are, I blinded myself to them, so that I would not be distracted.

I felt it most important, even at a very young age, to learn everything that he was there to teach me. That this opportunity was a once-in-a-lifetime thing, and sadly, it proved to be true.

I've never met anyone that possessed his incredible abilities to solve or fix any problem or challenge that came their way. He could make something literally out of nothing, taking what was legitimately trash and turning into real treasure well before he even turned sixteen! The man was limitless well before his time, and well before any movies ever came out bearing that name.

He taught us kids the ins and outs of wood, grains, care, sanding, restoring, and building. The laws that govern electricity and how to respect them so you don't get hurt, and possibly killed. The ease of plumbing and its remarkable simplicity. The intricate nature of automobiles and the com-bustion principles behind its propulsion. The wonders of welding, braising, and soldering, and of course fishing, and how to shoot the tiny lion off a Stroh's beer can from 40 paces.
The list of things that Dad taught us is endless and I find myself referring back to those things daily. In fact, it was Dad who first introduced me to photography, and nurtured it in me by passing down some old cameras of his. This is why there are very few photos of either him or me, and scarcely a photo of us together (beyond my wedding day) because one of us was always who was behind the lens.

The last photo I ever took of Dad was while he was sitting on the coffee table catching the news. I was standing in the dining room and yelled, "Hey Dad!" in order to capture him candidly, just as he taught me to.

Mailing a self-drawn portrait to Mom while actively serving in the war, Dad made a handsome groom (middle) and spent his remaining years, which ended just a few months shy of his 59th birthday, working hard. This is the last photo I ever took of Dad.

We were all truly blessed to have a genius as a teacher in oh so many ways. I think that is why it pained me so much to lose him, and in such a sudden and tragic way. I still can't even write about it here, more than forty-one years later, without tears pooling in the corners of my eyes.

I am so grateful that we all have so many happy memories of him that we can use to lean on whenever we start to feel sad.

I am not sure if Dad would tease us or perhaps test our loyalty, by telling us so called "secrets" that he didn't want Mom to know. One such "secret" only occurred when she left the house on Saturdays to go visit her sister and get her hair done. Once she had left, and he made sure the coast was clear, he would creep into her kitchen and cook up things for himself that he could stash out in the garage.

A no nonsense cook, Dad was always intent to make something that not only "hit the spot" and could "stick to your ribs" but also be able to be stashed away for later use, so Mom wouldn't know what he had been up to.

He was a big believer in having plenty to eat, perhaps because he lived through the Depression, and had experienced what true hunger felt like. I also think his cooking skills may have been influenced by being in the war and having to literally take care of himself in the field, living off canned rations, which he mentioned quite often while we cooked with him.

He'd often hard-boil eggs, a dozen at a time, then stuff them into coffee cans, which went wherever he'd go. When he cooked, aside from boiling eggs, he'd always use nothing but an old cast iron skillet that Mom didn't care too much for because she said its weight hurt her wrists.

I can recall one time in particular that he used it to show me and Nancy how to properly prepare beans and franks. Mincing onion and bacon very finely, then cooking them together until crisp, he then added thin slices of hot dog that he said were best when cut thinly because it lets more flavor get through.

Once the dogs were charred from the heat of the pan, he'd proclaim it time to pour in the can of beans, then christen the whole thing with a hearty spoonful of dark brown sugar because he said it helped add more richness to its taste. Stirring up the mixture with a big wooden spoon that he had hand-carved himself (for Mom) the flavor of his beans and franks was unforgettable and one that has stayed with this gal throughout life!

Daddy also liked potatoes to be cooked a certain way with his steak. A way in which he insisted that Mom use that cast iron skillet to make. Cooked over a high flame so the onions, bacon, and potatoes all got that cast iron char, the ingredients blended into a marvelous mix of flavors that were both savory and slightly oniony-sweet.

I loved the smell that Daddy's potatoes made and often tried to pinch some before Mom took him his plate!

Here's what's cookin' Beans & Franks
Recipe from Van Camps Dad Serves 2½
3T. chopped onion
2T. butter
1 15 oz can pork & beans
6 hot dogs, sliced penny size
⅓ c. brown sugar
1 slice bacon (cut into ¼" pieces)

Saute onions in butter w/ bacon in a skillet, until tender. Add sliced dogs & cook till lightly brown. Dump All into 2 qt. saucepan. Add pork & beans & b. sugar →

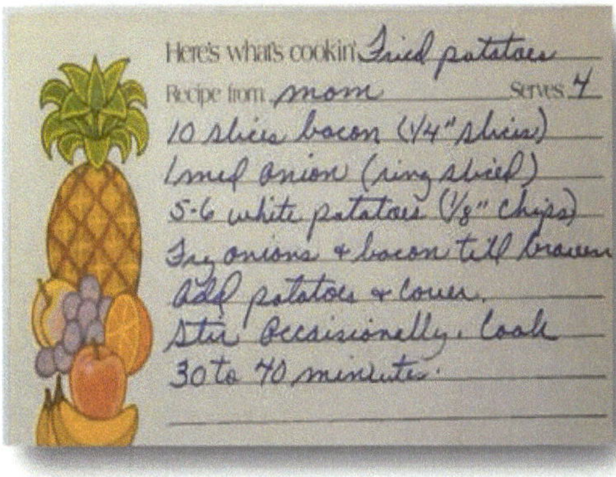

Here's what's cookin' Fried potatoes
Recipe from mom Serves 4
10 slices bacon (¼" slices)
1 med onion (ring sliced)
5-6 white potatoes (⅛" chips)
Fry onions & bacon till brown
Add potatoes & cover.
Stir occasionally. Cook
30 to 40 minutes.

Though I never saw Dad cook a single fish (that he caught or otherwise) and he caught hundreds, he did have cooking recommendations for them, with the top one being not to "cook" a fish at all, but rather just look to take the chill off its bones! This was his way of saying to go easy on the heat because it is easy to overcook a fish, which ruins its delicate texture, moisture, and flavor.

II

Family Favorites

With such a rich resource of recipes handed down to us from our "old country" ancestors, combined with the creative tendency that flows naturally through our Eastern European bloodline, it should come as no surprise that everyone in our household found time to tinker in either Mom's kitchen, Dad's "other room" workshop in the basement, or with him in the garage from time to time. With so many of us kids in the house I am sure that having extra hands to help out was welcoming so long as we didn't make too many mistakes, and made sure to hang those scissors back on the hook in the kitchen cabinet because that was their official place!

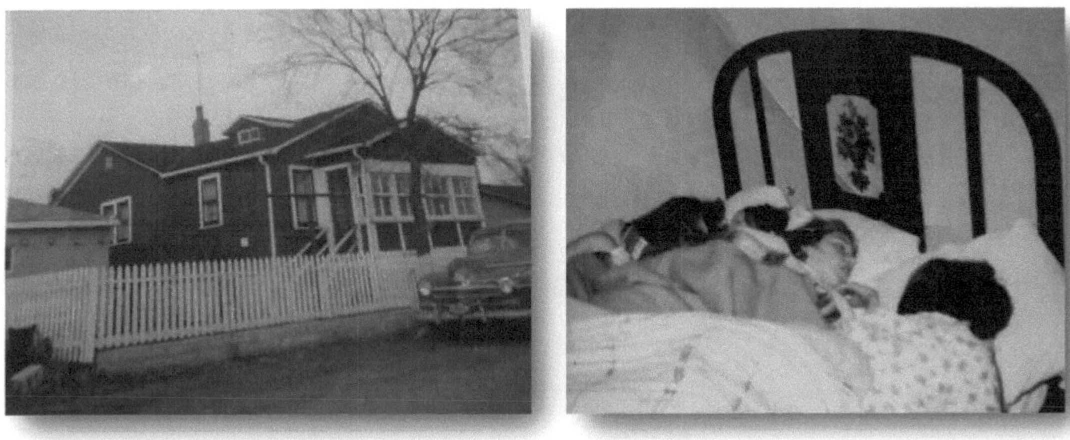

Our old family home was modestly surrounded by Mom's beloved white picket fence. Nancy, me, Diane, and Linda all shared the same bed for a time, and I can vividly recall waking them up in the middle of the night, begging them to get me a cold cup of milk. However, once they realized that bringing me that milk would cause me to wet the very bed that we all shared, my midnight milk wagon suddenly ran dry.

Dad was ahead of his time, not only in his genius abilities, but also in how he thought girls should be raised. In his mind, girls were no different than boys because as he put it, "Everyone needs to know the basics on how to care for themselves and their home." To know how to do things so we would not be dependent on anyone else.

He taught us all kinds of things and he turned everything into "teachable" moments long before that turn of phrase ever came into being and as we got older, Dad would teach us more in-depth things like oxy-acetylene torch capabilities. The smell his gas torch set produced was very distinct, and I discovered later in life that whenever I get a whiff of it, it pulls my mind's eye straight back to those days with him out in the garage!

Aside from the very tactile garage adventures Dad would provide, he would also present a series of on-going challenges for all of us kids to immerse our minds and/or bodies in. Challenges always seem to begin with an introduction because it was usually something new, then he'd present us with its challenge.

One time it was a glass quart-size mayonnaise jar that he had filled with coins. Our challenge was to guess how much money it contained. The prizes were sequenced so that all of us would win something, with the one closest to the actual amount getting the top prize. Even though we were kids and literally all we could do was take wild guesses, Dad still went to the trouble of stuffing a ten-dollar bill inside the cap to throw us off. Teaching us the lesson that in life there will be times when there is more than meets the eye.

He also challenged us regularly with mind-bending puzzles, and I specifically recall one puzzle that he challenged all of us to solve. He gave us all a full week to wiggle the puzzle around to master getting each ball in the right spot, but none of us could. At the end of the week Dad showed us how simple it was to solve. He set the puzzle on a flat surface then spun it round, employing the centrifugal force to each ball into each corner and solving this puzzle to the amazement of us all!

He also employed physical challenges as well, and one time made use of a pogo stick that I had bought myself with birthday money I received from my Aunt Marge. Dad gave us all one week to practice then come Saturday his official Pogo Stick Tournament began. Standing in a circle in the street in front of our house, Dad asked everyone when not jumping to count out loud while others jumped so we could keep perfect score. He gave us a short practice run then it was on to the official count, which would last until the jumper fell off. Their total would be tallied and then the next jumper would begin, and so on.

We all took his challenges very seriously, and I still distinctly recall sister Nancy winning this contest with well over five thousand (5000) consecutive jumps. In fact, I don't think Nancy ever fell off. Dad just simply told her she could stop jumping when it became obvious that Nancy was never going to fall off that pogo stick! I remember feeling proud of what I had jumped, but I can't remember how many, and being impressed by what the other sisters accomplished because everyone did amazingly well, but I think I remember Nancy's because we were all blown away by how she had truly become one with a pogo stick that day!
Nancy won the ten-dollar prize for being pogo champion, but Dad also handed me five dollars, too. Not as a prize (I bounced only 1100 times), but to replace my now worn-out pogo stick!

Dad also tossed in some plain old fun time too, which usually had an edge of danger that made Mom none too thrilled. For instance, because Dad was a tin smith he could make just about anything with metal, so he crafted us what he called a "flying saucer" which was a large curved piece of metal that looked like the top third of a giant globe. He would have us kids sit in it and then he would tie a rope from the saucer to his motorcycle then pull us around the park in the white, fluffy snow. We loved it, but Mom said she would be dying the thousand deaths if she had to watch us, so she would never go.

He also built, from scratch, both a motor home and a cabin cruiser to take us kids out camping and boating, respectively, and later bought an Amphicar, which neighbors still talk about to this day.

Letting us ride scooters and trail bikes, but only while we were under his supervision to meet Mom's demands. Dad had to enforce even stricter rules after I was hit by a car, an accident which resulted in multiple fractures to my femur, skull and jaw, but it happened while I was on my bicycle not the motorcycle.

To add some balance, literally, Dad had this exercise to do using books where he'd have us walk across the room while balancing an encyclopedia flatly on our head. He said it was to teach us to walk gracefully, like a young lady should.

For fun he would time us running up and down the stairs, and Margie was the fastest of us all because she could run down on all fours just as fast as she did going up.

He'd also make a game out of trying a new food, and I recall him offering us each a quarter if we would eat a sardine. Sister Diane was brave enough to eat it, but her stomach wasn't a willing participant. As a result, that tiny fish made a repeat appearance, which gained it one final "swim" in the toilet bowl!

Our parents also liked to weave in little, "old country" language lessons here and there. Dad taught us all to say, "Dobrú noc" which is "Good night" in Slovak, as we headed off to bed. He also taught us Dobré ráno (Good morning), and Dobrý večer otec (Good evening father), too.
I also recall, "My Boja, my boja," being said when something troubled them, not sure why.
Mom did some language immersion with us as well, deploying most of her favorite Eastern European catch phrases while cooking.
I recall her teaching us the word "Machanka," which she said was the name of a messy looking, unappetizing dish. She'd say, "Don't stir the chicken paprikash after adding the chicken because it will cause it to shred and look like a machanka." She'd also snap, "Stop being a sma-tee-kosh!" (phonetic spelling), which she said meant being a smart mouth, and if we were acting up, she would issue the warning, "Don't be a pee-Scott-tah!" (phonetic spelling) which she said meant being a pain in the you know what.
Dad was more inclined to scold us by saying, "Don't be a Dupa yash," which he said meant to be stupid or clumsy. He also said something to me that has stuck with me to this day, "There is a difference between being dumb and being stupid."

Thanks to an old neighbor, we also came to learn the term, "stati-babba" (phonetic spelling) which Mom said meant "mean old lady." She would use the phrase with a slight giggle behind it whenever the eldest woman in our neighborhood started yelling at the trash collectors for making too much noise while they emptied her trash cans.

Like most babbas in the neighborhood, we got to don our favorite "babushkas" as well. These were head scarves that in Eastern European tradition are often beautifully-made. In fact, while Mom was never big into clothing, shoes, jewelry, or accessories, she did have some precious and prized babushkas that she always cherished. It was the only clothing item I ever noticed being special to her, and she usually never left the house without one in tow. To honor that memory of her I keep a babushka of hers on my bureau near my bed.

Being orphaned by age eight, Mom said one of the things she loved about getting married was the bonus of getting a mother-in-law. A female that could teach her cooking knowledge and learn about recipes that Dad was fed. She was especially thrilled about this because she was raised by her elder brother, who taught her very little about cooking before she got married.

Sadly, our paternal grandmother died within a few months of their marriage so Mom got little time with her. She did feel blessed to have the time that she did because it enabled her to learn how to cook some dishes that were known to be some of Dad's favorites.

While I cannot recall all the recipes she learned from her mother-in-law, I do recall one that I came to love as much as Dad and that was Grandma Kurella's recipe for stuffing.

I loved the mere aroma of it as it was being made was so entrancing that Mom had to smack our fingers away. Talk about a memory worth savoring. I am so glad that Mom was blessed with the time she did have with Grandma Kurella because it enables all of us to honor her memory every time we make this recipe from Grandma Joanna.

Grandma Kurella's stuffing recipe, which likely from the "old country," continues to be a beloved family favorite, and one I sometimes make into mini muffins to bake fast. We are all ever so grateful that Mom got that chance to learn this recipe from Grandma Kurella because it enables us to enjoy it as well as pass it on!

Grandma Kurella's Old-fashioned Stuffing

This is an iteration of Grandma's recipe that Mom and I played with in the hopes of elevating it
Yield: 6 servings

1 pound of bread, cubed
1/4-pound bacon, finely chopped
1 large sweet onion, minced
1/4 cup butter
2 cups water
4 chicken bouillon cubes
1/4 teaspoon marjoram
1/8 teaspoon mint
4 eggs, beaten
Heat oven to 375 degrees. In large, deep, hot skillet over medium-high heat, brown bacon and onion with butter until very crispy and well browned. Add water, bouillon, and spices then simmer, stirring, until liquid is reduced to about one (1) cup of liquid. Remove from heat. In a large mixing bowl, toss cubed bread with beaten egg. Using a mixer paddle, or by hand, mix while slowly pouring the skillet mixture into bread, blending well. Add more bread if a drier consistency is desired or another beaten egg, if a wetter dressing is desired. Transfer dressing into a casserole dish or stuff into bird and bake for about one hour.
Alternate Method: Scoop mixture by tablespoon into a mini muffin pan sprayed with cooking spray. Bake for 35 minutes, or until desired doneness is achieved. NOTE: These freeze and reheat well, making this a great "make ahead" dish for the holidays.~

Through our childhood, Mom had a spice cabinet with three double decker lazy Susans in them to hold all her boxes, tins, and bottles of interesting things that we kids were never sure of. One spice that she held in such high regard that we were forbidden to even touch it because she said it was literally worth its weight in gold, was saffron. Bright red stigmas from the saffron crocus (Crocus sativus), the thread-like stigmas release their potent payload only upon being steeped in hot liquid. Mom always bought 1/4 gram packets of red threads and used it exclusively to elevate the flavor of her chicken soup!

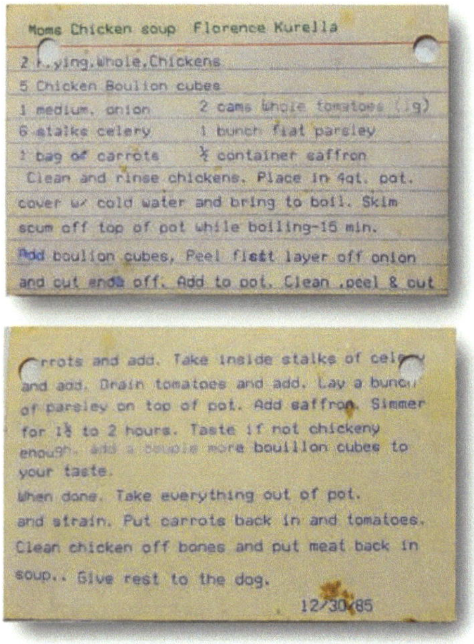

Moms Chicken soup Florence Kurella
2 Frying,Whole,Chickens
5 Chicken Boulion cubes
1 medium, onion 2 cans whole tomatoes (lg)
6 stalks celery 1 bunch flat parsley
1 bag of carrots ½ container saffron
Clean and rinse chickens. Place in 4qt. pot. cover w/ cold water and bring to boil. Skim scum off top of pot while boiling-15 min.
Add boulion cubes, Peel first layer off onion and cut ends off. Add to pot. Clean ,peel & cut carrots and add. Take inside stalks of celery and add. Drain tomatoes and add. Lay a bunch of parsley on top of pot. Add saffron. Simmer for 1½ to 2 hours. Taste if not chickeny enough, add a couple more bouillon cubes to your taste.
When done. Take everything out of pot. and strain. Put carrots back in and tomatoes. Clean chicken off bones and put meat back in soup.. Give rest to the dog.
12/30/85

Mom added the specialty, pricey spice, saffron, to her chicken soup, which adds a new depth in flavor profiles that this recipe simply cannot turn out right unless it is added. It also showed that Mom wasn't afraid to think outside her Eastern European spice rack to help elevate common recipes.

Mom's Hearty Chicken Soup (Reduced to 6 servings)

1-gallon clean water
1 whole (frying not stewing) chicken
3 bouillon cubes
15 ounces chicken broth
1 onion, chopped
1 turnip, chopped
2 small parsnips, chopped
2 pounds Roma tomatoes, quartered
6 leafy inner stalks celery hearts
1 bundle flat leaf parsley
1/2 teaspoon whole black peppercorns
1/2 container saffron (1/8 gram), divided use
2 pounds whole carrots, peeled and cut into 1-inch slices
4 Idaho potatoes, peeled and cubed
1 bag thin egg noodles

In a large stockpot, heat 1 gallon of water to boiling. Add chicken, bouillon, broth, onion, turnip, parsnips, tomatoes, celery, parsley, peppercorns, and 1/4 container of saffron. Bring to a boil and simmer for one hour. Remove from heat. Carefully remove chicken and place in a bowl then set aside. Strain solids from liquid. Skim off and remove excess fat, discard or reserve for a separate use.

Return strained liquid to stockpot and bring to a boil. Reduce to a simmer and add 1/4 container of saffron and carrots. Bring to a boil then reduce heat and simmer for 20 minutes.

Add cubed potatoes, return to a boil then reduce heat and simmer 20 more minutes or until carrots and potato become fork tender. Meanwhile, prepare the egg noodles according to package directions and clean chicken meat off the bones, moving to a separate, covered storage bowl. Finish straining remaining solids from initial boil, pressing through a large strainer.

Add the liquid to the soup pot and discard strainer contents or reserve for another use.

Once noodles are done cooking, rinse well under cold running water until cool and not sticky. Place noodles in a covered storage bowl and set aside.

Once carrots and potatoes are fork tender soup is done. Serve by placing desired amount of noodles and chicken in a soup bowl, then ladle soup with potatoes and carrots over them.

NOTE: I keep both the chicken and the noodles separate from the soup, adding it to the bowl only when serving because this keeps noodles and the meat from becoming water-logged, grainy, and mushy. ~

While Mom was a great cook, she had also clearly mastered the art of baking, and we, her children, were thrilled with the constant stream of confections she created! One confection that I was as fascinated by their creation as I was in eating them, were rosettes.

Transforming what looked like pancake batter into confections that are super light and crisp and cooked up real quick, this was one confection in the Kurella house that got eaten up lickety split!

According to some quick on-line research, rosettes are also called "struva"(in Swedish), of Scandinavian (Swedish and Norwegian) origin, and traditionally made at Christmas time. Using intricately designed irons that are heated in oil, dipped quickly into a simple batter then re-immersed into hot oil, crisping the cookie and releasing it from the iron instantly, these are such a delicious treat that our family couldn't stop eating them!

Made using common kitchen ingredients, the classic cookie-cutter shapes a rosette iron can provide, at an affordable price, are cute, but not necessary because batter can just as easily be poured directly into the oil to create unique, free-form patterns, which is where those funnel cakes come from! They can also be made ahead of time and stored (not garnished) in airtight containers - fresh or frozen - and then re-crisped in an oven for a few minutes before serving. However, you can't beat their fresh-made flavor so make ahead only if that is your only option.

When using a rosette iron, for best results be sure to maintain oil temperature by using a thermometer or an electric fryer. The iron needs to be just the right temperature for the batter to adhere and not stick or slide off. Be sure to dip your iron in the hot oil so it gets heated then remove and wait a couple of seconds for it to slightly cool, and then dip it in the batter.

This is a trial-and-error process, to gauge how long to wait so the iron will not be too hot. When dipping the iron in batter, be sure not to come over the top of the iron or the cookie will be difficult to remove. Be sure to drain them immediately on paper towel, clean newspaper, or clean brown paper bags.

To make sugar or other toppings adhere to cookie, sprinkle while cookie is still slightly warm. For a thinner, crispier cookie add a little milk for a thinner batter.

Store cookies in a tightly-sealed container or freeze them. There's no need to thaw them before serving. That said, nothing beats them fresh off the iron, so do try to make them just before serving if you want yours to be at their freshest best.

Mom's Swedish Rosettes

1/3 cup sugar
2 large eggs
1 large egg yolk
1 cup all-purpose flour
2/3 cup whipping cream
1 teaspoon vanilla
1/8 teaspoon salt
Oil for deep-frying
Powdered sugar

Beat sugar and eggs until well blended. Whisk in flour, cream, vanilla, and salt. Chill batter 2 hours or overnight. Heat oil and rosette iron to 365 degrees. Dip iron 3/4 of the way into batter, cook until golden brown. Approximate servings per recipe: 40. ~

Another holiday treat that wasn't from an Eastern European cookbook was Mom's cherry coconut bars, which holds a special meaning for me because it became the last recipe Mom posed with for my weekly newspaper food column, roughly two years before she passed in early 2014.

Exceptionally-flavored and offering her own signature melt-in-your-mouth buttery goodness, I can recall our Aunt Vickie always requesting a pan of them at Christmas. Aunt Vickie was married to our dad's brother, Uncle Kuzy. She was an angel (in a nurse's uniform) that served in WWII, and someone my parents both described as "One tough cookie!"

Thinking back to times when Mom would make them, I recalled how Dad, not wanting the juice in the empty maraschino cherry jars to go to waste, came up with an idea to mix it with milk for us kids (and himself) to enjoy as a special treat. I don't know if you have ever tasted such a concoction, but I can tell you that it is very similar to eating melted cherry ice cream, a special treat indeed!

Mom would always slice her bars on a diagonal to create perfect diamond-shapes and carefully trim away all the outer crust so that all pieces were identical. We kids loved that she did this because we got to dine on those cut-off, crusty edge rejects. In fact, if I close my eyes right now, I can almost imagine eating one…ah!

Mom's Special Cherry Coconut Bars

Yield: 24 bars

1/2 cup all-purpose flour
1/2 cup cake or pastry flour
1/4 cup powdered sugar
1/2 cup butter, softened
2 tablespoons all-purpose flour
2 tablespoons cake or pastry flour
3/4 cup cane sugar
1 teaspoon baking powder
1/4 teaspoon salt
2 extra large eggs
1/2 cup maraschino cherries, drained and chopped
1/2 cup sweetened, flaked coconut
1/2 cup finely chopped pecans
Garnish: Powdered sugar

Preheat oven to 350 degrees. Base: In the bowl of a food processor, combine flours and powdered sugar, mixing well then add butter in pieces and pulse until mixture resembles coarse crumbs. Press base mixture firmly into an un-greased 9-inch square pan then bake for 10 minutes. Meanwhile, in a bowl, combine flours, sugar, baking powder and salt. Add eggs, mixing well then stir in cherries, coconut, and nuts. Spread over pre-baked base then return to oven and bake for 30 minutes or until golden brown and center is solid. Cool completely on a wire rack before cutting. Sprinkle with powdered sugar, if desired. ~

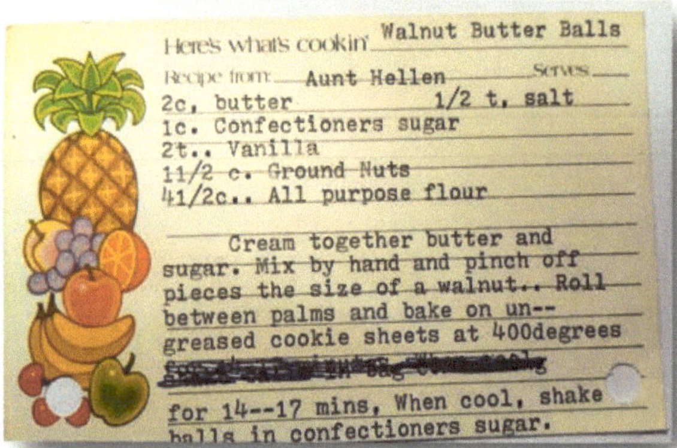
Here's what's cookin' Walnut Butter Balls
Recipe from: Aunt Hellen Serves
2c, butter 1/2 t, salt
1c. Confectioners sugar
2t.. Vanilla
11/2 c. Ground Nuts
41/2c.. All purpose flour

Cream together butter and sugar. Mix by hand and pinch off pieces the size of a walnut.. Roll between palms and bake on un--greased cookie sheets at 400degrees
for 14--17 mins, When cool, shake balls in confectioners sugar.

Finding this recipe card was a nice reminder of our Aunt Helen who was always sweet and kind and married to Mom's brother Art. Mom told me that this photo of her with her siblings was taken at my christening in July of 1961. (Left to right) Mom's sister, Marge, and husband Joe; Aunt Helen and Mom's brother, Art; Mom's sister, Jean, and her husband, Kenny; Mom's brother, Ed, and his wife, Jean; and Mom and Dad.

Mom was one of five children in her family, and with an older and younger sister, and two older brothers, she carried herself as the peace-maker among them. She practiced at keeping her head down, as she put it, to avoid any conflicts. She had confided to me that there had been strife between her siblings for some time, and though not saying why, she did reveal that this strife disappeared upon her giving birth to me because they all showed up for her at my christening. Mom confided that the photos from my christening were a happy reminder of her family's reunification, and of my birth too, of course!

I don't know if her brothers had any abilities in the kitchen, but I do know that her sisters, Marge, and Jean did because they would often bring us food or have us over. Aunt Jean and Uncle Kenny had the best parties at their house. It was always a pleasure to go there because they were so nice, and their daughters Kathy, Kay and Korky were also warm and welcoming whenever the Kurella herd would come stampeding in!

Aunt Jean ran a tight ship and her kitchen was no exception. Everything had its place, even a special closet where she kept board games to give us kids something to play with upstairs while the adults socialized in their awesome basement.

Uncle Kenny always kept a clean and well-stocked bar. Beautifully appointed, the wooden bar looked like it had been pulled straight out of an old saloon. Complete with a back bar featuring mirrors and clear glass door cabinets, Uncle Kenny had it bedecked with ornate and authentic bar lamps, which gave it an extra-classy feel. My sisters and I always felt special sitting at it and Uncle Kenny would kindly serve us icy glasses of 7-up with cocktail cherries on top!

I have sketchy memories of visits to Uncle Ed's, and the same is true of Uncle Art's and Aunt Helen's, but I do recall that Uncle Art was always very kind and Aunt Helen was, too. The same was true of Aunt Marg and Uncle Joe, a couple that seemed so in love their whole marriage through. Unfortunately, I do not have recipes from any of them, except for one, which leads me to think it must have been a pretty special one.

Dad liked to infuse thought-provoking statements throughout our childhood. He must have figured that we'd eventually encounter things in life that would cause his wisdom to be triggered in some way like a trap that catches a mouse, only in a different sort of way. Dad once said, "If everyone you knew got together in a circle and placed their problems out so everyone could see them, everyone would pick up their own problems and walk away." Being young at the time, I did not fully grasp this statement's meaning, but once I got older and began to hear of other people's woes I sure did!

Another parable he told that still haunts me to this day is: "I cried because I had no shoes until I met a man who had no feet." At the time he told this to us there was a man in our community that, for whatever reason, not only had no feet, but also no legs. The man would transport himself in a special wheeled, wooden cart that was fashioned to fit him perfectly. Using wooden pegs that he would whip against the sidewalk for traction, the man seemed to have no trouble propelling himself forward considering his drastic disability.

In time Dad's parable caused me to visualize that man whenever I began to pity myself. In his own way Dad was saying, "Sure, we can all find an excuse to complain or cry, 'Poor me!' but in truth there is always going to be someone out there that has it far worse than you or me!"

Dad's infusion of this wisdom in childhood helped to teach me how to stop feeling sorry for myself. That "pity parties for one" do nothing but sink you lower than you were when you began, and they inflict personal harm. Fighting the tendency to sink into a negative state is no easy task, but both Dad and Mom taught us that we should, like the much-loved Monty Python lyric states, "Always look on the bright side of life," and in our family home there was no quicker path to "happy" than through food. In fact, it reminds me of another phrase Dad used to invoke quite often while eating and that was, "We may not live in a castle, but we sure eat like kings!"

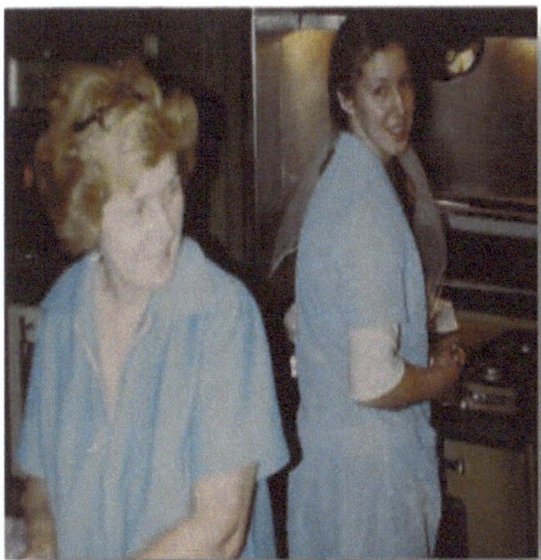

Here's whats cookin' Fudge Cuts
Recipe from Mom Serves
2 sqs. Chocolate. ¼t. salt
½c. shortning ½c. flour
1c. sugar 1t. vanilla
2 eggs beaten ½c. nuts
Melt Choc,+ shortning. R.F. H.
Blend in sugar,eggs, + flour.
then salt. Stir well. Add
vanilla. pour in 2 8x8x2" pans.
Spread smooth + sprinkle w/ nuts.
Bake 400* for 12 min. Cool ,cut
into 2" sqs. Makes 32 cookies.

Mom (with Nancy) would occasionally surprise us with what she called "keeper" recipes. She made a bunch of this fudge one year and I ate so much I made myself sick. It was a while before I could eat fudge again.

Having the esteemed title of being both the eldest, and only brother among seven siblings, brother Tom had a catch phrase that none of us will ever forget.

"Mother, the girls are laughing at me!"

An artistic soul, Tommy's creativity shows itself through mind-bending art, music, and also his deep and abiding love for cooking.

The eldest, and 11 years my senior, I have no memories of Tom cooking until we were both adults. A natural cook who also gets lost in the process of creating, Tom's "MacGyver" talents are widespread like that of Dad, who could pick up any instrument and immediately play it by ear. Self-taught in many things, Tom's love for music, art and cooking have always been the hallmarks in his life.

Tom's Stuffed Pepper Soup

1-pound lean ground beef
1 large onion, 1/2-inch dice
1 cup uncooked rice
1 (15.5oz) can Hunts red pepper and fennel diced tomatoes
1 (15.5oz) can tomato sauce
1 teaspoon dried oregano
1 teaspoon basil
1/4 teaspoon pepper
32 ounces chicken stock
2 tablespoons powdered beef stock
3 large green peppers, 1/2-inch dice
4-5 red and 4-5 yellow mini bell peppers, 1/2-inch dice

Over medium heat, brown beef, and onions. After the meat has cooked through, add rice and brown slightly. Add into the pot: diced tomatoes, tomato sauce, oregano, basil, salt, pepper, chicken stock, 2 cups water, powdered beef stock and bring to a boil. Reduce heat to simmer, cover and allow to cook for 20 minutes. Add peppers and cook another 30 minute or until rice and peppers are tender. ~

Tom's Tetrazzini

2-3 cups cooked diced meat (turkey, chicken, veal, shrimp, beef)
1/4 cup butter
1/2 teaspoon white pepper
12 ounces chicken broth
1 can cream of chicken soup
1 cup half & half
2 tablespoon white wine
1 pound cooked spaghetti
8 ounces sliced fresh mushrooms
2 tablespoons capers, chopped
3 ribs celery, 1/4 inch dice
1/2 cup onions, chopped
1/2 - 1 cup parmesan cheese, grated (enough to cover top of the baking dish)
1/2 teaspoon paprika
parsley to taste

Microwave celery, mushrooms and onions on high for 6 minutes, meanwhile, melt butter in a sauce pan, add flour a little at a time until a paste forms. Mix in salt and pepper. Slowly whisk in broth, a little at a time, until fully incorporated. Add cream of chicken soup and boil 1 minute. Remove from heat, mix in wine, spaghetti, meat, and vegetables. Pour into a large baking dish, sprinkle top with grated Parmesan and paprika. Cover and bake at 350 degrees for 1 hour. Remove foil and brown top of casserole. Serve with a green salad and crusty bread. ~

Getting assistance from daughter, Kayleigh Erin, to provide his recipes, Tommy and the rest of us have come to realize, especially with the passing of two of our very dear siblings (in as many years) that it is vital that we do take the time to write down recipes, so that we can pass them down to be savored by future generations- just as our ancestors did for us!

Tom's Meat Loaf

1 pound each, ground beef, veal, and turkey
2 bell peppers, 1 red, 1 green
1 large onion, diced
8 ounces fresh mushrooms, chopped
1 can diced tomatoes, rinsed, and drained
15 ounces seasoned breadcrumbs
1 jumbo egg

Mix and form a loaf. Put into a greased 8X10 or larger pan and bake at 400 degrees for 1 and 1/2 hours. Spoon off grease, pour tomato sauce over the top of the loaf and cook an additional 30 minutes. Serve with mashed potatoes and sweet corn. ~

XII
IX
III

When I think of Jeanne, I immediately recall her meatloaf, which she revealed was a recipe from the back of a canister of Quaker oatmeal.

Jeanne also made a killer stew that was so good that I would request her to make it as payment for babysitting.

In later years, Jeanne got into soups and zucchini breads because she was growing them in her garden.

Her enthusiasm for life, no matter what was going on, was infectious and one of her most redeeming qualities was her generous heart that used her gifts to bless others through sewing, crafting, cooking, and keeping your taxes filed on time!

Because of the ten-year age difference (the same I share with my husband), I had no memories of my dear, recently departed sister, Jeanne, cooking in the kitchen until she returned to the Calumet Region as a wife and mother in the early 1970s.

Jeanne was a "Flower Child" from the 1960s and had this free-wheeling vibe that never quit. She was very creative and with thread being stitched into the Kurella bloodline as much as was gravy, she was drawn like a moth to the flame into the world of sewing and mending, which flowed naturally through her fingers as a gifted seamstress.

Like Dad with his torches, Jeanne could do almost anything with a needle and thread. Demonstrating that same "MacGyver" limitless potential he harnessed, albeit through thread. Jeanne's brain never quit stitching up creative ideas that she chased, literally, with a needle of some kind and a thread, until we lost her on her 72nd birthday.

Surrounded by family as she drew her final breaths, we sisters decided to joyously sing our family's favorite religious version of "Happy Birthday" to her so that Jeanne could hear all our voices and know she was not alone as she made her big journey from this life to the next.

"Happy birthday to you. Happy birthday to you.
Happy birthday dear Jeanne, happy birthday to you.
Many more birthdays to you, many more birthdays to you.
Many more birthdays dear Jeanne, many more birthdays to you.
This is Jeanne's birthday, happy, happy birthday. We sing 'happy birthday' to you today.
May Our Lady bless you on this happy birthday, may Our Lady bless you on every day!"

Then, as we shouted and clapped each of her years, *"One (clap), two (clap), three (clap)..."* all the way to seventy-two as Jeanne passed peacefully into the loving arms of Our Lord.

Thinking of Jeanne's cooking, I recall her meatloaf, which she revealed was a recipe that came from the back of the Quaker oatmeal canister that she "doctored" with lots of extra onions. She also made this killer pot roast/stew that I would request as payment for babysitting for her if that tells you anything. In later years, she got into soups and zucchini breads to make good use of the things she grew in her north Hammond garden, which were simply awesome, too.

Jeanne's Savory Slow-cooked Pot Roast/Stew

2 pounds red meat (favorite source)
1/2 cup all-purpose flour
2 tablespoons extra virgin olive oil
1 large onion, diced
2 pounds whole carrots, peeled and chunked
2 cups low-sodium vegetable broth
4 medium -large red skinned potatoes, washed and cubed
2 bay leaves
1/4 cup Worcestershire sauce
1 teaspoon black pepper
1 tablespoon celery flakes
1 tablespoon thyme
1 teaspoon sweet paprika

Cut meat into bite-size pieces, then place in a bag with flour.
Shake to evenly coat.
In a large skillet over high heat, heat oil.
Add onions and cook, stirring, until they begin to caramelize, about 7 minutes.
Transfer onions to crock pot, draining oil back into skillet.
Add floured meat to hot skillet and sear on all sides.
Once browned, add to slow cooker, draining oil back into pan.
Add carrots to skillet and cook, stirring for about 3 minutes.
Pour broth into skillet and, using spatula, scrape bottom and sides of skillet to deglaze, loosening browned bits from pan.
Pour all into crock pot then to crock pot add potatoes, bay leaves, Worcestershire, and spices.
Stir to mix then cover.
Set crock pot to "low" to cook for 8 hours, or set it to "high" to cook for 4 hours.
Remove bay leaves before serving, or leave them in and play the game that whoever ends up with the bay leaf in their bowl doesn't have to help clean up! ~

Jeanne's Zucchini Nut Bread

1 cup grated zucchini
1 egg
1/2 cup honey
1/2 cup oil
1-1/2 cups all-purpose flour
1 teaspoon cinnamon
1/2 teaspoon baking soda
1/4 teaspoon baking powder
1/2 teaspoon nutmeg
1/4 teaspoon finely shredded lemon rind
1/2 cup chopped walnuts*

Preheat oven to 325 degrees. In a large bowl, beat together zucchini, honey, egg, and oil. In a medium size bowl, combine flour, cinnamon, baking soda, baking powder, nutmeg, and lemon peel. Slowly incorporate flour mixture into zucchini mixture. Fold in walnuts. Grease an 8 1/2" x 4 1/2"x 2 1/2" loaf pan. Pour bread mix into pan and bake until toothpick inserted in the center comes out clean (about 60 to 70 minutes) Cool on wire rack. *= I swap out the walnuts for 1 cup fresh or frozen blueberries (pictured). Yield: 12 slices ~

Jeanne's Creamy-Cheesy Broccoli Soup

1/2 cup chopped onions
1/2 cup chopped celery
2 tablespoons butter
2 cups chopped broccoli
4 cups water
4 chicken bouillon cubes
8 ounces cream cheese, cubed
16 ounces real sharp cheddar, cubed
2 tablespoons sour cream
1 can cream of chicken soup

Sauté onions and celery in 2 tablespoons butter. Add broccoli and cook a minute or two until color changes. Add water and bouillon cubes. Cover and cook until broccoli becomes tender, around 20 minutes. Add cream cheese, cheddar, and sour cream. With a wire whisk, blend in the cream of chicken soup, whisking until it begins to boil. Remove from heat and serve. Yield: 8 servings ~

Every memory I have from childhood of sister Margaret is sugar-coated because she was (and still is) an upbeat person who is always smiling, usually optimistic, and always ready to cook something up in the kitchen!

She's also not afraid to spend too much time there either. On the contrary, she puts so much time and attention into her cooking that she should have gone to chef school!

I love the sweet memories I share with her and I am thrilled to have her still present to contribute her favorite recipe, which is her American Potato Salad. A dish that she has been making since she was a kid!

Memories of my sister Margaret (aka Margie, Maggie or even just Marg) cooking in the kitchen seem to lean more toward baking delights in the oven than cooking on the stove, but it is likely due to my young age when she was still living at home.

Margie dabbled in just about everything, making amazing salads, sides and mains, like Haluski, but if I had to pick, I think I favored her sweets over anything because she always did something to elevate them to a higher level, such as her pumpkin pie, which she elevates by adding more spices, which give it more "zing" than your average pie!

Margie has always been a sweet sister. She brought me burgers from the Corral where she worked while I was an invalid convalescing from the auto accident, which, after six weeks of traction that had me literally tied to a hospital bed, transitioned to a body cast for another six weeks as well. Her surprising me with a burger from the Corral was often my only happiness during those lonely, isolating and painful days of recovery.

Reflecting on childhood, I have a memory of amazingly-light, sweet and crispy krullers (pro-nounced "CRA-lures") that Margie used to make. I remember watching how she would slit the dough and pull part of the dough through the hole so that it gave it a unique shape, and then toss it into the Dutch oven filled with shortening. The aroma that plumed into the air was sweet and inviting and their light, sweet, crispy-warm and delicious taste was enough to make you smile!

The pleasure I felt in tasting these long-forgotten childhood treats makes it well worth the flour-coated counter it will create, and if you have a pasta roller it makes it much easier to get the dough thin and uniform, too. In fact, not only does it roll the dough perfectly thin and make it easy to handle, it also gives you another way to make good use out of that old pasta machine, too!

Margie's "MacGyver" truly comes out in the kitchen, but there was always one dish she was best known for making, even in childhood, and that was her potato salad. Implementing her penchant for tinkering with recipes, Marg has perhaps spent the better part of her life applying her own kitchen kaizen to this dish, tweaking it beyond the limits that most other cooks would ever dare to tread.

Always wanting to make it the best that she could, Marg has most definitely conquered the art of creating the best American potato salad there is, and with all the work she has put into this recipe, if we could give her a potato crown it would be one that she earned the right to wear most deservedly.

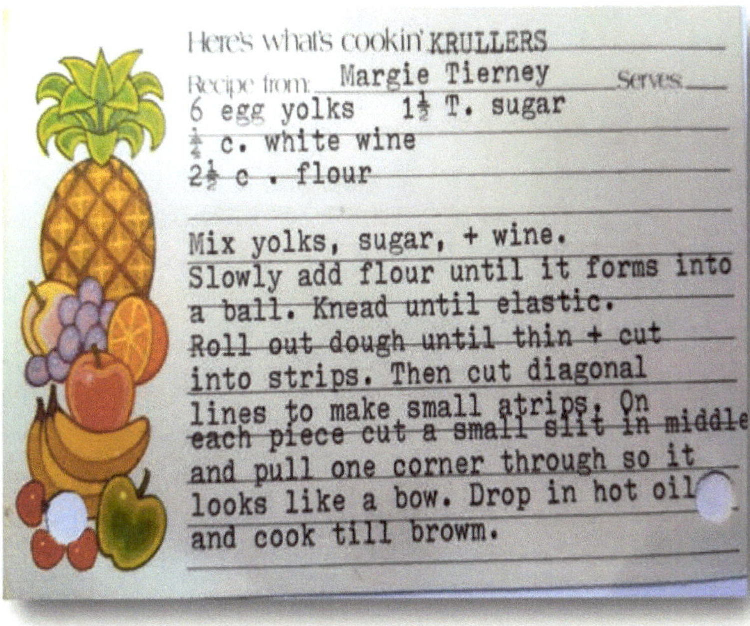

Here's what's cookin' KRULLERS
Recipe from: Margie Tierney Serves:
6 egg yolks 1½ T. sugar
¼ c. white wine
2½ c . flour

Mix yolks, sugar, + wine.
Slowly add flour until it forms into a ball. Knead until elastic.
Roll out dough until thin + cut into strips. Then cut diagonal lines to make small atrips. On each piece cut a small slit in middle and pull one corner through so it looks like a bow. Drop in hot oil and cook till browm.

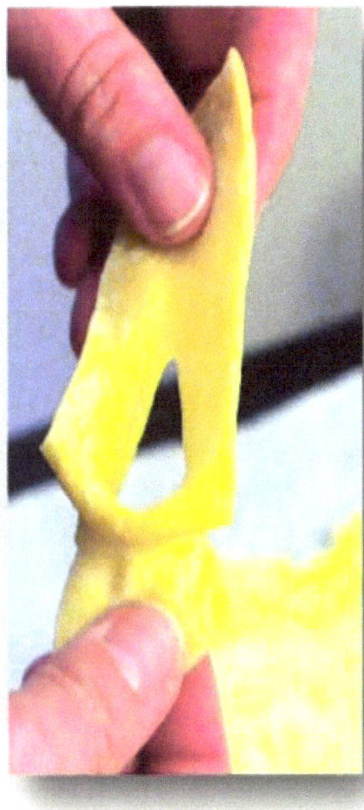

Maggie's Potent Pumpkin Pie

Yield: 8 servings

1 9-inch pie shell, unbaked, in pan
1 egg white, lightly beaten
2 cups pumpkin
1 cup packed dark brown sugar
2 teaspoons ground ginger
2 teaspoons ground Saigon cinnamon
1 teaspoon fresh grated nutmeg
1/2 teaspoon ground cloves
1 teaspoon salt
2/3 cup heavy cream
2/3 cup milk
4 large eggs

Lower oven rack to lowest position and heat oven to 400 degrees. Prepare piecrust for blind baking (prick bottom with a fork, line crust with parchment and fill with dried rice or beans). Bake crust for 15 minutes. Remove parchment from crust, prick any bubbles with a sharp fork and bake shell for 8 to 10 minutes longer, or until bottom just begins to color.

Remove crust from oven and brush lightly with egg white while still hot. Process the pumpkin, spices, and salt in a food processor for 1 minute. Transfer mixture to a 3-quart heavy saucepan. Bring it to a simmer over medium-high heat. Cook pumpkin, stirring constantly, until thick and shiny, about 5 minutes. Whisk heavy cream and milk into pumpkin mixture and bring to a simmer.

Process eggs in food processor until whites and yolks are mixed, about 5 seconds. Gradually pour hot pumpkin mixture through feed tube while processor is running.
Pour warm filling into pie shell. Shield crust edges and bake 25 minutes. Filling will be dry looking and lightly cracked around the edge. The center will wiggle when pie is gently shaken.
Cool on a wire rack.~

Maggie's Marvelous Potato Salad

2 pounds red potatoes, boiled to fork tender, cooled, peeled, then cut into cubes
6 hard-boiled eggs, peeled and cubed
1/2 cup green onions, sliced and slightly chopped
1/2 cup dill pickle, sliced medium thick, then cubed
3/4 cup mayonnaise
1/2 cup sour cream
2 to 3 teaspoons bottled yellow mustard (optional)
1 to 2 tablespoons dill pickle Juice, or to taste
salt and pepper, to taste

Put all potatoes, other vegetables, and eggs in a large bowl. Combine the mayonnaise, sour cream, pickle juice and mustard, if using. Add to potatoes and gently combine potatoes, vegetables, eggs, and mayonnaise dressing. It is delicious as is, if it seems like it needs a little more dressing, add a little more of the mayonnaise and sour cream. Chill for 3-4 hours for flavors to develop.~

Our "rebel" with a cause, sister Linda took time away from her heavy study load to take Dad's Honda 90 Trail bike out for a spin.

A "book worm," as Dad affectionately called her (because her face seemed buried in books), Linda's "MacGyver" intelligence grew with studying and eventually lead her all the way to attaining her Ph.D.

"Great job, Linda!"

Looking back, I seem to recall sister Linda having quite the knack for anything sweet, and I hold a very vivid memory of an angel food cake she once made from scratch that she drizzled with a chocolate sauce that was the best I ever ate!

I don't recall if it was for an occasion, but I do recall that it was the first time I had ever tasted an angel food cake, and boy, was it divine! Linda had done such a wonderful job that her cake seared itself into my memory. So hard, in fact, that I cannot look at or even think of angel food cake without recalling hers. Her cake has become the standard by which all other angel food cakes are measured against!

Intimidated by how careful Linda was, which included issuing a "no running or jumping in the house" edict for fear her cake would fall, I put off baking my own angel food cake for fear of failure until I was well into my middle ages.

A book worm and voracious reader, Linda was also a curious adventurer in our youth. She was not afraid to take her curiosity into the kitchen, especially once she began taking a course in French language while in high school.

Using her sisters to help her learn this second language, Linda bought these cool little French phrase books for us to attempt to speak to her in French and help her to become more fluent in the language. Mind you, I was ten at the time, so the language was a barrier, but in helping her learn I became a sponge and began to pick up a little of that language, and as a result, decided to take French when I went to high school!

With Linda immersing herself into the French language, her interests began to widen into all things French it seemed. I didn't mind helping her learn the language by running cue cards with her or practicing phrases, but I can tell you that I absolutely loved it when she brought her new love for all things French into the kitchen.

I still can't help but issue forth a pleased sigh just thinking back to her immersion in French cuisine. I can't honestly say which recipe I liked most among them because they all left me with such pleasant memories.

I recall the time she attempted to replicate the French crullers we'd buy fresh from the local donut store. I distinctly remember them because while they may not have looked donut case perfect, their flavor was simply off-the-charts divine! That experience had a profound and lasting impact on my palate, teaching me that all donuts, especially French Crullers, are not created equal.

Linda demonstrated that not only is it possible to make donuts like store brands, but also better. It was a lesson that, even though I was a kid, was not lost on me. Along the way I picked up some donut-making tips, as well:

1. DO use a fat that is solid at room temperature, such as vegetable shortening. Donuts fried in a fat that is liquid at room temperature like canola oil, soy oil or any other liquid oil will make your donuts VERY greasy, resulting in excessive fat absorption and not so great donuts.
2. DO use all-purpose flour. Bread flour or self-rising (unless called for it) will make donuts tough and chewy.
3. DO use real butter, when called for. Margarine, substitutes or spreads often contain high amounts of water and other compounds, which can have less than desirable effect on your end result
4. DO use eggs, when called for. Crullers depend on the egg to rise as lightly as it does. Using a substitute can lead to disastrous results.

She may have not realized it at the time, but Linda also taught me a VERY important lesson about donuts that still stick with me to this day, and that is that doughnut not freshly-made is a donut not worth eating.

I also have a sweet memory of a time Linda had me help her make crepes to take over to the convent for a special meal with the nuns there. Of course, Linda had to spend time perfecting her French crepe recipe and I gladly volunteered to be her guinea pig because she was stuffing them with amazing fruit fillings- hello!

That time with her became another sweet memory that I still have resurface whenever the occasion for crepes come along!

Linda's Awesome Angel Food Cake

Yield: 12 servings.

2 cups egg whites, room temperature
2 teaspoons cream of tartar
2 teaspoons pure vanilla extract
2 cups cake flour
2 cups white sugar
1 teaspoon natural fine sea salt

In the bowl of a mixer, beat egg whites until they form stiff peaks, and then add cream of tartar, and vanilla extract. In a separate bowl, sift together flour, sugar, and salt. ⊠ sing a sifter or a slotted spoon, thoroughly combine dry ingredients.

Reduce mixer speed to slowest setting and add dry ingredients a half-cup at a time, then pour completed batter into an un-greased 10-inch tube pan.

Place cake pan in a cold oven. Turn oven on; set temperature to 325 degrees. Let cake bake for 1 hour, or until cake is golden brown.

Remove from oven and invert cake – turn upside down- and hang on a heavy wine bottle to allow it to cool in the pan.

Once thoroughly cooled, remove from pan. ~

Chocolate Glaze (Optional)

2 cups powdered sugar
1/4 cup unsweetened cocoa
2 tablespoons water or cold coffee
1 teaspoon pure vanilla extract
3 tablespoons butter, melted

In a small bowl, whisk together powdered sugar, cocoa, water or cold coffee, vanilla, and butter to make a smooth, pour-able glaze. Adjust wet and dry ingredients to reach desired viscosity. Pour the glaze over the cooled cake. Let the glaze set for 1 hour before serving.~

Linda's Incredible Crullers

1 teaspoon sugar
1 cup boiling water
1/2 cup butter
1 cup sifted all-purpose flour
4 eggs
1/2 teaspoon pure vanilla extract
vegetable shortening for frying
2 cups powdered sugar
1/4 cup milk or cream
dash of pure vanilla extract

In a 2-quart saucepan, bring sugar, water, and butter to a boil. Using a whisk, add flour and beat vigorously over direct heat until mixture becomes very thick and leaves the sides of the pan. Remove from heat and whisk in eggs, one at a time, beating hard after each addition. Add Vanilla then beat mixture until gloss disappears. Heat vegetable shortening to 365 degrees. Force mixture through pastry tube l or through a doughnut maker plunger onto greased paper. Carefully turn paper upside down over pot so crullers will drop into hot shortening. Turn crullers as they become lightly brown, about 30-40 seconds. Remove and drain on absorbent paper. Make glaze by stirring together the powdered sugar, milk, and dash of vanilla in a small bowl. Drizzle over crullers.

Yield: 24 crullers. ~

Linda's Classic Crepes

Yield:12 crepes

1 3/4 cups whole milk

4 large eggs

3 tablespoons extra light olive oil

3 tablespoons granulated sugar

1 cup all-purpose flour, measured then sifted

oil or butter, greasing pan

In a bowl, combine eggs, oil, sugar, and milk. Add the flour to the mixture and mix again until all the flour is incorporated. Run crepe batter through a sieve. Grease the skillet with butter, oil, or baking spray. Once the skillet is hot, turn heat to medium/high. Pour about 1⊠4 cup of the crepe batter into skillet and swirl around the skillet so the batter is evenly spread in skillet. Once the bottom of crepe is golden, flip the crepe and cook until bottom is golden. Repeat with the remaining ingredients. ~ **Custard Filling**

1 tablespoon all-purpose flour

1/8 teaspoon salt

1 cup whole milk

1 teaspoon pure vanilla extract

1 teaspoon cornstarch

1/2 cup granulated sugar

3 large egg yolks

whipped cream and berries (optional)

In a bowl, combine flour, salt and cornstarch. In a saucepan, whisk together egg yolks, sugar, milk, and vanilla. Over medium heat, bring to a boil. Add dry ingredients to pan and whisk vigorously until well incorporated. Turn heat to low and continue cooking until custard thickens. Remove from heat. On a crepe, add custard filling, roll tightly, repeat. Then add a topping, if desired.

Sister Diane was not in the kitchen that much when I was a kid (as I recall) but chances are it was because the older sisters and Mom always were, and there was simply no room for us three little kids, as she, Nancy and I were called. However, I do have a memory of me getting to help her make a dessert salad for Easter, and it may have been an annual thing, but at this point due to aging, my recollections are starting to slip. Mom called the dish a Hawaiian salad and said it was named that because it had coconut in it, but we just called it "Good!"

I especially liked the canned fruit that went into it, and enjoyed having the job of opening and draining the cans because it gave me the opportunity to help myself to a few mandarin orange slices and pineapple tidbits before I passed the drained cans on to Diane.
It's funny, but recalling it right now is enabling me to picture, in my mind's eye, the two of us standing in Mom's kitchen back then. With me at the sink draining the cans, and Diane to my right, mixing up this salad, there was a sweetness in the air that we both loved. Good times! Honestly, I am surprised that Diane let me handle the cans at all given my history of dropping food, which I'll tell you about later.

Today, Hawaiian Salad, or Ambrosia if you prefer, has been transformed into a dish that has become more like a diverse fruit salad and less sickly sweet through the swapping out of ingredients, which does change its taste. Being traditional, our family likes to stick with one of Dad's favorite rules and that was "If it ain't broke don't fix it" and according to our fond childhood memories of this dish it's one that will never be broke!

Diane married into a polish family, which influenced her cooking thanks to guidance from her mother-in-law. Combining her own "MacGyver" traits, which inclines her to tinker with things, Diane combines life experience with her own ingenuity to repair and upcycle all kinds of things, most especially those old Polish dishes that her unique tinkering takes to greater heights!

With the spirit of a firecracker, sister Diane is a cook that prefers no nonsense.

Often relying on a pressure cooker or crockpot to do the heavy lifting, I can thank Diane for teaching me the importance of inspecting a pressure cooker before use, and making sure you don't go above the "max" line in the pot.

Like the dog-butter story about me, I 'll never forget the time that Diane blew up the pressure cooker cooking dog bones in Mom's kitchen.

It sounded like a bomb went off, and all of us were afraid to go to see what happened.

When Mom went in the kitchen all I could hear her saying was, "Oh my goodness!"

Strong and determined, Diane always gets what she sets her mind to done! God bless her!

Diane's Authentic Polish & Kraut

2 pounds fresh-smoked Polish sausage
1 large jar or bag sauerkraut
1 large yellow onion, chopped
16 ounces diced tomatoes
1 teaspoon garlic powder
2 to 3 dashes black pepper
2 cups water

In a crockpot, combine sauerkraut and its juice with tomatoes, onion, garlic, pepper, and water. Mix well then slice smoked sausage into 1/4-inch pieces (if using) and stir. If using fresh polish, simply place sausage on top of mixture to rest. Cover pot and cook on "high" for 3 to 4 hours. Check sauerkraut. When it becomes as tender as you like it, reduce pot setting to "low." Remove fresh sausage (if using) and slice then return to crockpot.

Circling back to why I was surprised that Diane trusted me to handle food when I had a history of dropping it, revolves around a story that Diane loves to tell about me from childhood, when I was likely around five or six years-old. I dropped a stick of butter while trying to liberate it from the refrigerator and our small terrier dog, Princess, quickly snatched it and dashed to hide under the dining room table.

Sisters Diane and Nancy witnessed the whole thing and quickly scolded me, saying that I was going to get into big trouble because the butter was going to make the dog sick. Filling me with panic, I quickly scrambled under the dining room table and pried the jaws of this little dog open with my tiny hands, which was an effective way to wrestle that stick of butter away from the dog.

Snatching it back quickly, I ran it into the kitchen where the light revealed it had been badly pierced by the dog's tiny teeth and had some of its hair in it as well. Showing it to my sisters one of them replied, "You're gonna have to clean that all off or you're going to get in big trouble because butter is expensive."

The only way I could figure to clean it was to run it under the water in the sink. It works on dishes, why not butter, too?

Running it under hot water looked to wash all my problems away, but when I went to dry the stick of butter (with a towel) the linen fibers began to adhere, so I had to rinse the butter off again. I must have washed and tried to dry that stick of butter quite a few times before Diane and Nancy finally intervened. Laughing, they told me not to worry about it, then grabbed that stick of butter and walked away. I never got in any trouble, so whatever they did must have worked, and I learned a valuable lesson that day, which was while you can wash butter, it's almost impossible to dry it, too!

Diane's Favorite String Bean Soup

Yield: 6 servings

1 pound bacon, chopped

1 large sweet onion, chopped

6 cups water

1/4 cup white vinegar

3 teaspoons chicken bouillon

4 (14 ounce) cans of French style green beans*

16 ounces sour cream

3 to 4 large russet potatoes, peeled and cubed (optional)

*= 2 pounds of fresh green beans can be "frenched" and used, but cooking time is longer.

In a large pan over high heat, fry bacon till super crispy. Add onion and cook until it begins to caramelize, about 7 to 8 minutes. Transfer mixture to a large soup pot. To empty skillet, add water and swirl to pick up errant bits, then pour over bacon mixture in pot and set skillet aside. To soup pot, add vinegar, bouillon, and green beans. Bring to a boil, then reduce heat to a simmer and cook for one hour. Add potatoes and cook until fork tender, about 15 minutes. Taste and add more vinegar if desired. Heat sour cream in the microwave for 1 minute. Stir then heat for 1 more minute or until it gets very warm, or it will curdle. Once cream is hot, stir into soup. If using fresh beans, cook until beans are tender.

Diane's Delightful Old-fashioned Hawaiian Salad

Yield:12 servings

16 ounces sour cream

20 ounces canned pineapple tidbits, drained

7 ounces sweetened flaked coconut

10 ounces miniature marshmallows

30 ounces Mandarin oranges, drained

In a large, non-metallic mixing bowl, combine sour cream, pineapple, and coconut, blending well. Add marshmallows, mixing well, then fold in oranges gently so they don't fall apart. Cover well then chill overnight or at least 8 hours before serving. ~

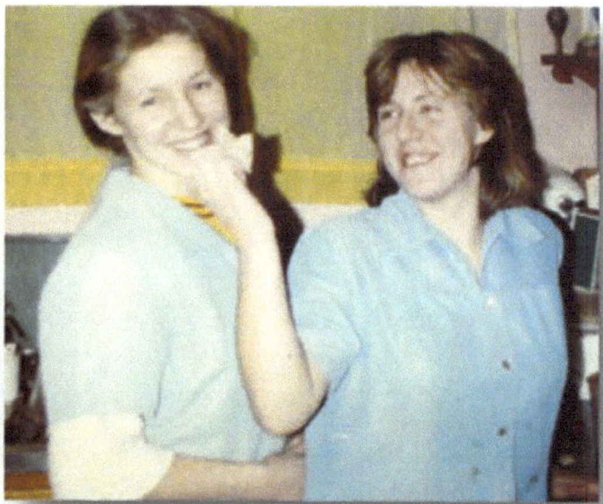

Because you almost never saw the two of them apart, Mom referred to Diane and Nancy as "Frick and Frack," the famous comedic ice-skating duo popular in the 1930s.

Caught playing in the bathroom mirror (left), Diane and Nancy would make funny faces for each other in an effort to crack each other up under the guise of a dare.

Remaining close, even though they grew up and eventually developed independent interests and their own circles of friends, the "Frick and Frack" in Nancy and Diane (right) continued to make special appearances all the up and until Nancy passed into the arms of Our Lord shortly after her 62nd birthday in 2020.

A happy spirit, Nancy found great joy in cooking and loved to host get-togethers, especially potlucks, which enabled everyone to taste each other's latest experiments.

The last few times we got together were under such circumstances. Sharing food with each other always made our times together unique, a little adventurous, and a delicious and heart-warming way to touch base.

A strong woman with a resilience that I personally admired, Nancy was a force to be reckoned with. She was someone who always worked very hard and made it a point to achieve everything that her heart desired.

My being the youngest sibling made Nancy the closest in age to me, just three years my senior. While she did spend lots of time with Diane in her younger years, once Diane got into her teens Nancy gravitated toward me, which was helped by Mom, who wanted Nancy to chaperone me after that car accident thing. Problem is we were kids, so we continued to inflict i njures. I slipped on rocks and fell in deep water. I fell through the ice on the lake while we were ice skating. Luckily Nancy was there to save me both times. I 've slit my toes open to the bone due to tripping over hunting knifes at my childhood best friend, Cindy Boguszewicz's home. (A brother who hunted would always have a knife stuck in the ground somewhere for gutting things.)

My foot was impaled by roofing nail that made one of my sisters say, "Trying to be like Jesus?"

I've been hit in the head by a football field sprinkler head, and still have a dent in my head to prove it, and quite mysteriously, I got a huge chunk of muscle and flesh severed from my left leg, but have no memory of how it happened. It was weird because Nancy and I were just playing in our yard.

Judging by the size of the scar (I still have) there must have been a big chunk of my little leg out somewhere in our little yard, and I bet you the dog found it and ate it!

Nancy and I had lots of less dangerous times, too. In fact, my first "adult-free" c ooking experience occurred when I was with her. We used to pack up a bag and pretend we were going on an expedition like the guys on Animal Kingdom. We'd grab a can of string beans, some butter, two forks, a can opener, and a pack of matches then stuff it all into a small paper bag. When we did this, it meant we were going for one of our long walks, which was all the way out to Swarthouts, and about a mile or so away from our home, which was perched near the shores of Wolf Lake.

Once we'd get to the other side of the lake we would walk along the water's edge to our own private place that had this huge cottonwood tree that we built a ramshackle of a treehouse in. Nancy would instruct me to gather some twigs while she arranged stones to place our little fire in, and once our tiny fire got going, Nancy would have me open the can of beans and drain it. Then she'd put some butter into the can, remove its label and then set the label in the fire and place the can right on top of it.

There on the water's edge, with the fresh air causing the Cottonwood's leaves to wiggle in the breeze, we would eat string beans straight out of the can while it sat over our tiny fire.
While it may not sound like much, to us it felt like a wilderness adventure and we loved that feeling oh-so-much!
I learned from this first culinary experience too, that beans over an open fire will more often than not be so hot that they are almost guaranteed to burn you!

Nancy loved to cook, and she was very good at it, too. In childhood she was the noodle queen because Mom said she ate more noodles than anyone else in the family. Perhaps this was a mere foreshadowing of the pierogi princess she later became. I can still recall how excited she got while taking home economics class. Her enthusiasm was so infectious that it drove me to take it, too.

Getting herself a little metal recipe card file to stash her recipes in, Nancy was so obsessed with keeping it orderly that she would scold me and even slap my hands if I ever got near it.
Nancy used her "MacGyver" strengths to attain all the goals she set her mind and heart to.

One recipe I recall her loving oh-so-much was a dill dip. She even prepared it lovingly and shared it by pairing it with our favorite crudités: Cauliflower and carrots!

Here's what's cookin' DILL DIP
Recipe from: NANCY GORMLEY Serves:

1 1/3 c.Hellmans mayo
1 1/3c. sour creme
1T. parsley flakes
1T. dill weed 1t. Bon appetite (mc Cormick Brand)
Mix all ingredients together at least two hours before you plan on serving.

Striking a pose with Nancy, while I was 9 years-old and in a body cast, and she about 12, I will never forget the joy that recipes and cooking brought Nancy, nor will I never forget the joy that her recipes, like this Dill Dip, and her presence in our lives brought to us. She is unforgettable!

Nancy was a baker and a cook, and I think she enjoyed both equally, and was just as fascinated as I was when we'd get to try out a new recipe. I remember the first time we tried to make turn-overs, a recipe she got from class at school. We tried using jam as filling and there ended up being more jam on the pan than in the turnovers! We used a butter knife to scoop the filling back in and then made extra glaze to cover up the fix, which prompted Dad to say to us, "Do you know the difference between an amateur and a professional?" and we said, "No."
He replied, "The difference is that a professional knows how to hide their mistakes!"
Thus giving Nancy and I the nod on how we "fixed" them!

Nancy's Tempting Strawberry Turnovers

1/4 cup granulated sugar
2 tablespoons cornstarch
1/4 teaspoon salt
1 tablespoon water
2 cups chopped rhubarb
2 cups chopped strawberries
1 tablespoon orange zest
2 sheets of frozen puff pastry thawed
1 egg slightly big beaten
1 cup powdered sugar
1 to 2 tablespoons of water
1/4 teaspoon of pure vanilla extract

In a 2-quart saucepan, combine sugar, cornstarch, and salt. Stir in the one tablespoon of water then add the rhubarb. Place pan over medium heat and cook stirring occasionally until rhubarb is tender and the liquid has thickened like a jam.

Remove from heat and let cool for 30 minutes. Once cooled, stir in strawberries and orange zest.

Preheat oven to 425 degrees. Line two baking sheets with parchment paper. Unfold a puff pastry sheet on a lightly floured surface then cut each sheet into three rows. Then cut on long end to create three equal size squares.

Roll each of the squares into approximately a 5-inch square. Turn the square on an angle and egg wash the two front edges then place a spoonful of the fruit filling in the middle of each square.

Fold the top portion of the triangle over the bottom portion of the triangle then, using the tines of a fork, press to seal the edges together to seal.

Slit the top of the dough to create steam holes then place turnovers on the prepared baking trays and place in the freezer for 10 minutes.

Remove the pans from the freezer and either wrap each turnover for long-term storage in the freezer, or brush the tops of the turnovers you plan to bake with the beaten egg, and a sprinkle of sugar, if desired.

Place pan in oven for 5 minutes then reduce oven temperature to 350 degrees. After 15 minutes of baking time has passed rotate pans and then continue to bake for 10 more minutes or until turnovers puff up and are golden brown.

In a small saucepan over low heat, whisk together powdered sugar water and vanilla until smooth. Add more water or powdered sugar to reach desired viscosity.

When turnovers have finished baking, drizzle the warm glaze generously over each turnover.

Nancy's Petite Pies

All-purpose flour, for rolling
2 packages of refrigerated pie crust (3 crusts needed for this recipe)
1 egg
1 tablespoon of granulated sugar
1 pound of rhubarb cut into half inch pieces
1-pound strawberries hulled and cut into half inch thick slices
1/4 cup granulated sugar
1/4 cup light brown sugar packed
3 tablespoons cornstarch or arrowroot powder
Zest from one lemon
1 teaspoon pure vanilla extract

Preheat oven to 400 degrees. Roll out three pie crusts into 12-in rounds. Using a 4" circle cutter, cut circles of dough. Place 4-inch circles into the bottom of a muffin tin cup, keeping the top edge of the dough flush with the top of the cup. Repeat. Use remaining dough to cut 4-inch long by 1/2-inch-wide strips then set aside. In a bowl, combine rhubarb, strawberries, sugar, brown sugar, cornstarch, lemon zest, and vanilla. Mix well then fill each cup with 1/3 cup of the filling. Use the dough strips to form a lattice crust on top of each pie. Use fingers to connect lattice crust to bottom crust. In a cup, blend egg with one teaspoon of water then lightly brush the tops of each pie and sprinkle with a little sugar. Place in the oven and bake for 23 to 25 minutes or until the filling begins to bubble and crust becomes golden brown. Remove from oven, Cool for 15 minutes before serving. ~

Through the years of my siblings generation.

The greatest prize in life is family, and all the blessings that ancestors, parents, siblings, spouses, children, grandchildren, aunts, uncles, cousins, and extended loved ones (adopted or otherwise) can bring. It is because of the "bread crumbs" they leave us that we have such a flavorful family history, which enables me to convey my life through all these wonderful recipes.

I've learned so much through life, and one of the most profound has been that words like "mother" or "father" or even "sister" or "brother" are not the nouns we assume them to be. In truth, they are job descriptions that deserve to be placed upon those who do the work, if you know what I mean.

Blood, while it has its place, is just a fraction of who we are. In the end, it takes a lot of different people to help us bring out the best of who we can truly be. It is a blessing (not a curse) to have so many others in your life. Never forget that.

My hope is that you enjoyed this flavor-filled journey through our family's generations and it inspires you to cook a few of their recipes that come from different places and directions.

Following the beat of your own drummer is something that makes us all unique. I feel blessed that my children and grandchildren all march to their own beat. It is a sign, as Dad would say, of "MacGyvers" in the making!

Witnessing the grandkid's kitchen prowess at such young ages makes me feel confident that those coming up the ranks will have enough culinary experimentations to fill a book of their own some day. Perhaps one they will let me help create!

Given the flavorful foundation from which they all spring, I might even venture to say, "The best is yet to come, baby!" and I hope God blesses me with a front row seat to see it!

FYI: Everyone who walks the earth has a "MacGyver" in them in varying degrees. To call it out all one needs to do is something that brings joy to them and others, then lean into it!

May Almighty God and your own powerful "MacGyver" force always be with you!

The next two generations of my branch of the family tree.

III

Calumet Region Cuisine

In 1851, the first of three rail lines, Michigan Southern Railroad, laid its tracks across this wilderness, and by 1871, with the installation of a post office, the area's moniker got shortened from Pop Whiting's Siding down to just Whiting, and according to an 1880 census, 115 people were residing there.

In the 1870s, when the federal government built a harbor for the Calumet River, steel mills began to flock to the Chicago area. In 1889, the Standard Oil Company began buying up land along the lakefront, and by 1895 Whiting was incorporated as a town, then went on to become a full-fledged city in 1903.

By 1923, the Standard Oil Company's refinery employed over 4,000 workers, causing the city's population to expand toward 10,000. Mark Manufacturing Co., aka Indiana Harbor Works, Chicago Heights Steel, and U.S. Steel were also busy providing job opportunities that promised high wages, which became the catalyst for all our grandparents to immigrate to America and head straight for Whiting. The place where my parents would eventually meet.

Mom began working at Standard Oil's candle factory during WWII, a time when women were called into the work force to help the war effort. She regretfully noted that once the men started returning after the war had ended, women were asked to give up their jobs so that the returning men could resume work, and that she was ultimately asked to quit her job upon marrying Dad because married women had no reason to work back in the 1940s.

Because the area was such a melting pot, drawing multiple ethnicities in for the work, the city became heavily dotted with both taverns and churches. In fact, I can recall someone once saying that there's a tavern or family market on just about every corner and a church on every other block!

According to the Whiting-Robertsdale Historical Society, at its peak, the Whiting-Robertsdale community did have around 25,000 residents, and while most were Roman Catholic, many were also Protestants, Jews, or following a non-denominational religion, so yes, there were churches everywhere in this small community.

It always puzzled me why such a small community needed five separate Roman Catholic churches all less than a mile apart. Apparently it was due to the area being flooded with a mixture so ethnically diverse that not all Catholics spoke the same language. Therefore, five separate churches were necessary so that Mass could be spoken in the different languages being used. It also says something that such a small town could support that many churches, too. That's a lot of Catholics!

St. John's Roman Catholic Church

American Slovak Club

St. John was Slovak as was Immaculate Conception. St. Adalbert was Polish, Sts. Peter & Paul was Croatian, and Sacred Heart was Irish, giving everyone a church they could hear Mass spoken in their native language.

The dozens of taverns and bars were also a result of the language barrier issue. That and the huge number of workers that rotated on twenty-four-hour shifts, making it very lucrative for taverns to serve food and drink around the clock.

Since there were thousands of workers, there needed to be plenty of places to accommodate the hundreds that would get off from a shift all at the same time.

What's interesting is that some of these taverns got so good at cooking that they developed a following. In fact, there were lines forming on Fridays, a day in which this heavily Roman Catholic population ate fish. The best places in town (in my childhood) included Kay Ann's, Cellar Tap, Dusty's, and Center Lounge to name just a few.

Dusty's Tap

Just Dotty's

Diamond Tap

As of this writing, there is just a handful of Whiting-Roberstdale establishments left to go to for an adult beverage, and the tradition of a Friday fish fry is still alive and kicking in at least at one establishment there: Center Lounge.

CENTER LOUNGE (1910-present) has seen many changes in ownership over its very lengthy history, but its doors have never stayed closed. As a result it has earned the esteemed distinction of being not only the oldest establishment in town to still have its doors open, but also one of perhaps few that still offer fresh-cooked fish come Friday.

Still serving fish on Fridays, the Center Lounge in Whiting, located on 119th Street, has become one of the area's oldest and most treasured venues that you can still frequent for food and drink to this day.

Doing some non-expert research on the subject of taverns and bars in the Whiting-Robertsdale area, which included asking people on social media and listening to a funny original song written about this very subject, "Drank in Every Bar" by Bill Y Lee (in 2018 according to YouTube), I was surprised to learn just how many different establishments have come and gone. So many, in fact, that I needed an EXCEL spreadsheet to track them all down!

This made me realize two things: The old cliche was true, there were taverns on almost every corner- through time!

I thought it might be fun to make a game (for those familiar) out of trying to recall where these places used to be, which ones replaced each other, which are still around, and how many you can (honestly remember) and check off the list as places you've been.

Past + Present Establishments in Whiting-Robertsdale

This list, which numbers 117, represents the names of drinking establishments that local people were able to recall. As a result, it may not be fully accurate, so my apologies in advance. Many of these establishments did share the same address over time, which was due to changes in ownership over the course of 119 years that Whiting has been a city. In the end, my tally appears to reveal that the Whiting-Robertsdale area looks to have gained a new place to go to almost every year! I created this chart for those who want to play "Match Names with Places" or perhaps check off places you have been.

	1 & 2		Gyures		Paradice
	5 Points		Halupki Inn		Parkview
	9 to 4 Tap		His & Hers		Pat's Tap
	A & H Tap		Hob Nob		Phil Smidt's
	Al Knapp's		Hoosier Tap		Piggy's
	Amvets		Jakes's Tap		The Point
	Andy Peters		Jean's Tavern		Portside
	Bar Rio		Jen's Apartment		Refinery
	Beggar's		Jerome C's		Robertsdale Inn
	Bercik's		Jerry's		Roby Tap
	BJ's		Jewel Tap		Roosevelt Club
	Black Steer		Jim & Jan's		Rose & Onnie's
	Bootleggers		Jim's Saloon		Runicks
	Brownie's		Just Dotty's		Sally's
	Bulldog		Juster's Steakhouse		Sand Bar
	Bucky's		Kay Ann's		Sandy's
	Cafe Roosevelt		Kidtown		Selo Lounge
	Captains II		Klens		Skip's
	Carl and Billy's		Knights of Columbus		Slovak Dome
	Center Lounge		Keith's		Sokol Club
	City Lights		Koval's		Someplace Else
	Chuck's Tap		Leisure Time		Spebars
	Clipper		Left Guard		Spicca's
	Club Neon		Leslie's Tap		Sportsman's Corner
	Condes		M & M Lounge		Standard Tap
	Country Junction		Margaret's		Townhouse
	Cousins		Mark's Tap		Tumble Inn
	Cozy Tap		Mary Prices		Turtle Bar
	Curly 'N' Johnny's Dugout		Mom's Bar		Twilight Zone
	Diamond Tap		McHales		Up for Grabs
	Dew Drop Inn		Midtown		VFW
	Double Z		Moose Lodge		Vodka Room
	Elks Club		Mr. Ed's		Vogel's Viking Room
	Emil's Tap		Nardi's		Volders
	Four Deuces		Nasty Habits		White Oak Lounge
	Franky V's		New Yorker		Willows Tap
	Game Time		Nite Life		Woodrow Wilson Club
	Good Times		Navotny's		Y-Not
	German Fun Club		The Office		The Zoo

One place that I would be remiss not to mention in the same breath as Whiting-Robertsdale's fish fry is not a tavern, nor in Indiana, but a place many residents still flock to (any day) because it's just down the road. Located literally on the edge of the 95th street bridge, on the southeast side of Chicago, a bridge made famous when the Blues Brothers jumped it in their movie. Calumet Fisheries is not your average fish place, but neither is what they serve.

Opening in 1948, brothers-in-law Sid Kotlick and Len Toll created Calumet Fisheries (CF) to fulfill a dream to serve the freshest, tastiest specialty fish on the South Side. 65 years later, CF is still run by the Kotlick-Toll families and remains a strictly a take-out business run out of a tiny building with no seating, and no bathrooms. It does offer a great view of the water and the bridge that you can enjoy while dining on their specialty fish in the comfort of your own car, though!

Reflecting on childhood, which had no bars or taverns in it (unless there were family parties and events we were taken to), I feel extremely blessed to have lived in a place where a kid could safely wander the entire place on foot.

As a child, the lure of sweet-smelling penny candies that perfumed the dry air in all the small Mom and Pop markets had no trouble pulling us kids right in. I can almost remember the exact treats that each store would have, too.

I was in love with shoe string licorice, and do recall loving those flying saucers filled with tiny beads because they offered a strangely similar texture and taste similar to the communion wafers we got at church, but they came with the bonus of candy inside.

I recall walking up 119th street, which took us past Condes Deli. Offering candy of course, but even at our young age we came to appreciate it more for its awesome fish, chicken and coleslaw that they served at their hot food counter in the rear. Sister, Nancy taught me how to order there, which was to tell them how much money you wanted to spend on food. She'd say, "I'd like a dollar's worth of fish to go," and they would scoop out a portion of fish and cook it up on the spot then pop it into a paper bowl and slip it into a white paper bag then write on it how much to charge us with a grease-stained pen. We'd grab a bottle of soda to split, hit the front counter to pay, then head outside to the front of the store and rip open the bag and gorge on those piping-hot filets! We'd often combine our alfresco dining at Condes with window shopping at Rudolph's beauty shop next door.

Some days we'd hike up 119th a little further and hit White Castle instead, especially if we needed a restroom break or to warm up our cold little hands. Looking back, I think candy was the main reason that we never made a trip downtown without stopping at the Taxi Stand or the Whiting News Co., which offered the biggest and best selection of penny candy in the land. It's a wonder my teeth didn't rot out with as much candy as we used to eat.

We also almost always crossed the street and headed into Newberry's, so we could shoot to the back and check out the pets. Some days we'd sit at the soda fountain counter and watch them cook those amazing grilled cheese sandwiches on their hot, ever-sizzling grill, some days we got lucky enough to order one to split, too.

On rare occasion, we would pop into Ralphs Restaurant and order something small to split, like an order of fries and a soda, but more often than not we'd spend most of our time hanging out at the Community Center either taking lessons in their swimming pool or learning to play ping pong with some newly-made friends. There were also times that Mom gave us a list and some money to pick up special items from Weiner's, a grocery store that Mom fancied most for a few specific deli items that she adored.

After burning off so much energy at the Community Center we'd be starving and pinch pennies in the hopes of being able to slip into Ande's for one of their amazing beef sandwiches.

ande's pizza

OVEN HOT DELIVERY—CARRY-OUTS

Dial 659-3078

OPEN 4-12 DAILY—4 PM-1 AM FRI. & SAT.
1309 COMMUNITY COURT Closed Mondays
Across From the Community Center in Whiting, Indiana

Pizza
Broasted Chicken
Shrimp *Lake Perch
Roast Beef
*Friday Only

Cheese	$ .90	1.40	1.75
Sausage	1.25	1.80	2.50
Anchovies	1.25	1.75	2.10
Green Peppers	1.25	1.75	2.10
Sausage with Green Peppers (or) Mushrooms (or) Anchovies	1.55	2.10	2.75
Sausage With Green Peppers Anchovies & Mushrooms	1.80	2.75	3.25

Any Combination Made to Order (As You Desire)

Hot Roast Beef Sandwich on Italian Bun .50

FROM OUR FABULOUS BROASTER

BROASTED CHICKEN—All Our Chickens Are Prepared Daily and Broasted To Order In Our Kitchens . . . Disjointed For Ease in Eating

Half of a Chicken, Broasted to a golden brown, with cole slaw, french fries, roll and honey	$1.45
2 pieces of delicious Chicken Broasted to a golden brown, with french fries, cole slaw, roll and honey	.90
Large super Shrimps with cole slaw, french fries, shrimp sauce, roll and honey	1.35
Golden brown fresh Lake Michigan Perch fillets with tartar sauce, cole slaw, french fries, roll and honey	1.00
Box of Broasted Chicken (10) pieces with french fries	2.50
Box of Broasted Chicken (20) pieces with french fries	4.75
One pound of large super Shrimps	2.25
One half pound of large super Shrimp	1.25

SIDE ORDERS

Tartar Sauce	5c	Cole Slaw	15c
Shrimp Sauce	5c	French Fries	25c
Rolls and Honey	25c		

All Orders Plus Tax

When we were at home, Mom would treat us on occasion to pizzas from the Barany-owned Dino's, which was just down the block from home.

In 1964, Mr. Barany became a co-owner of Dino's Pizza, then two years later he became sole owner. Dino's remained in the Barany family until they sold it in 1982.

I loved Dino's throughout my childhood. I adored their special Italian sausage recipe, their special sauce, and how delightful their cracker-crisp crust always was. The Barany Family knew how to make an insanely-good pizza, and ruined me for life because all pizza I eat is automatically measured against theirs. I miss those guys! [FYI: Dino's did re-open with new recipes and It's one of few left for pizza that's well-worth going to!]

In my travels the closest I can come to the Barany-owned Dino's pizza flavor is at House of Pizza. I have to order extra sausage and then its taste "hits the spot!"

As a kid, the only other pizza place we frequented was Shakey's in Highland. Loving their "all you can eat" buffet which had these awesome little, cinnamon-spiced apple pies that were a little bigger than a tater tot; Shakey's Spuds, which tasted like batter-dipped and well-seasoned penny-sliced potatoes that were fried to a perfect crisp exterior that gave way to a moist and creamy center.

Well-known for pizza, chicken, and uplifting ambiance and occasional piano man that banged out roaring sing-a-long tunes, Shakey's offered an ambiance of an old saloon and was always so packed I was surprised when it closed.

Then there were those times where Nancy would get a bug to take a walk down Indianapolis Boulevard, sometimes to pop into White Castle and say, "Hello!" to our Aunt Marge (pictured) and then head northwest toward Illinois, which usually meant she had a taste for Arnie's, which offered the best hot dogs and Polish in town. [FYI: Arnie's is still there and nothing about it has changed since we were kids!]

Art's Drive-in at 5 Points in Whiting, IN

Margaret Hmurovich at Whiting White Castle

We'd walk a little further, just to catch a glimpse of all the action at Art's Drive-in then turn tail and head home. If we had a dime between us, you could almost guarantee we'd be stopping by Merry Isle for a cone for us to split on the way home. Nancy would eat it down to the cone then hand it to me to finish because she liked the top and I liked the cone!

NOTE: I sourced information from an admittedly brief search on the internet as a way to offer some tidbits about these places for the unfamiliar. Unfortunately, not every place has information available, so what is written reflects what I could find or my own personal knowledge and experience. All establishments that appear are here to reminisce not to promote or advertise. I received no payments or compensation from anyone to mention them in this book.

As I grew older, I came to experience the more mature restaurants in our area, like Spiccia's, which offered fine Italian dining right across from Wolf Lake.

On the far north end of town, which shared borders with the south side of Chicago and Lake Michigan, there was a small string of restaurants to suit your pleasure and pocketbook, including Art's Drive-in, Al Knapp's, Condes Restaurant, Vogel's, and of course the world-famous Phil Smidt's!

SPICCIA'S (1941-1995) was an old-fashioned Italian opened by restaurateur, Mike Spiccia. It was Whiting's only Italian eatery (that I recall) in its day which set it apart from the others. Featuring straw-covered Chianti bottles that were used as candle holders over and over until wax covered just about everything, Mr. Spiccia decorated the place well in Italian everything. Using Italian red and green as his theme, he accented with tiny white lights that helped to illuminate the dark wood and give the textured walls a glow that made you almost feel like you were transported to Italy when you were inside this restaurant's walls.

Owner, Mike Spiccia believed that everyone who dined at his establishments deserved VIP treatment, and between his outstanding food and service there was nary a disappointed person in the crowd.

I remember going to an event there when I was just a little girl and found it so enchanting that I didn't want to leave. In later years I had the pleasure of dining there and my goodness was I pleased. He offered unusual selections, and one I've never seen before or since and that was a wine-marinated Michelangelo steak and what he called the pizza steak, which was smothered in mozzarella and tomato sauce-oh my! I suspect that Spiccia's closed its doors when Mr. Spiccia passed away.

Spiccia's Dining Room in during the 1980s

CONDES RESTAURANT (1950-1990) initially started when the four Condes brothers, George, Peter, Sam, and Chris opened Condes Drive-Inn in Whiting. In the early 1960's Condes Restaurant on Indianapolis would open. Later adding a banquet hall and catering facilities (and my favorite childhood deli on 119th), the brothers kept themselves very busy with food and by the mid-'80s, between banquet halls, college concessions and truck stops, the brothers were juggling seven independent operations.

I recall great lunches and dinners there in my early adult life during the early 1980s. The great service and its ambiance, which reminded me of an old supper club, which I adore. I can still re-member how delicious their filet mignon was, too. Talk about a memory worth savoring... Mmm! Sadly, with times changing, so came the eventual closing of its doors.

VOGEL'S (1921-1997) was initially opened at 2501 Calumet Avenue in 1921 by Fred and Ida Vogel, and offered a capacity to serve 100 customers.

Operating there for about a year and a half, until it was completely destroyed by a fire, with no insurance to cover it, they relied on help to rebuild, which eventually expanded them to seat an impressive 450 guests.

Business continued to be prosperous until around 1938 when road changes reduced traffic flow, and triggered them to move the restaurant to a busier street. This is how 1250 Indianapolis Boulevard got to become its new address.

Taking about six years to fully build, the grand opening took place in August of 1944, and opened with a capacity to seat 1000 guests. Offering a supper club-like setting, and featuring signature dishes such as frog legs (that came from frogs the family raised themselves), Shrimp de Jonghe, steaks and of course, boned and buttered lake perch.

Coming to be appreciated for both its fine dining and as a place for upscale showers, banquets, wedding receptions, after earning the title of being the oldest family-run restaurant in the area, and an impressive seventy-six-year run, the Vogel family closed its doors for the last time in 1997.

I fondly recall their amazing service, their super-chilled relish trays, and their moan-worthy Shrimp De Jonghe, a dish I loved so much that I had to conjured up a recipe to make it at home for myself. (Look for it to appear just a little bit later in this book!)

PHIL SMIDT'S (1910-2007) Started out with a $600 loan taken on May 30, 1910, by Phil and Marie Smidt, to open a bar and restaurant that offered a 12-seat, three table dining room and 12-foot bar with an attached boat livery. Marie's special recipe for pan-fried perch, served "all you want" with rye bread and a vegetable for 40 cents turned out to be such a hit that the Smidt's repaid the loan in just 59 days!

With Marie passing in 1926, Phil married Irene, who helped him grow the restaurant at its height to an impressive 450 seats! The restaurant's notoriety grew exponentially as well, attracting people from all walks of life, including actors like James Cagney, Bob Hope, Frank Sinatra, Babe Ruth, Jack Benny, and perhaps most notably the Prince of Wales, who is now the King of England, and Mom once thought she figured out their secret: Butter!

As all good things do eventually come to an end, Phil Smidt's closed in October of 2007. After an impressive 97-year run, I count myself fortunate to have dined there on more than one occasion. I distinctly recall the last time I was there because it was to attend the funeral luncheon of our much-loved Uncle Kenny, God bless him!

Mom and I did play around in the kitchen trying to recreate Phil's recipes, and I'd have to say we got it as close as possible to the real thing by mixing cracker meal (no longer exists) with some seasonings then frying the fish in a pan filled with a puddle's worth of hot, melted butter. It was good!

[FYI: I heard through the grapevine that Phil's did rely on the flavor of butter to elevate the food they served, but they did so by using butter-flavored oil to fry everything in.]

Sadly, there are no restaurants left in the Whiting-Robertsdale area that offer the lineage of these old greats, but if you happen to be in Whiting and you want to get close to that old-fashioned quality, service, and taste, then I would go to Keith's, a little Whiting restaurant that serves up big city quality and taste!

KEITHS (1990-present) was opened by Scott Keith, a local podiatrist who wanted a restaurant that offered the kind of food he found in downtown Chicago closer to home, so he created Keith's!

Offering actual tablecloths, which is becoming scarcer these days, I personally think that they add that special touch, some comfort, and a classy feel that elevates the ambiance in their small dining room. Featuring a handsome, retro-style wooden bar that exudes a masculine presence, like a guard standing watch, the contrasting modern open-kitchen concept adds a delightful animation to the room and the air, filling the space with its awesome aromas and the visual excitement of flames that dance according to how the chef conducts them.

The menu is small, but smart and special, with offerings of steaks, seafood, pasta, and specials that rotate. I've dined here on many occasions and have always found everything to be great, and I like their blend of both old and new, which works well in their small, quaint, intimate space.

HOUSE OF PIZZA (1954-present) is just outside of the Whiting-Roberstdale area, but within the Calumet Region and it's one of a handful of places that you can still be served old-fashioned great taste. House of Pizza serves honest-to-goodness authentic, from-scratch-made dishes using their family's own, "Old Country"recipes!

Dante Zunica first opened House of Pizza in 1954, using his grandmother's "Old Country" recipes. Still operating out of its original location, with Dante's grandson now supervising, House still cooks their pizzas on a circa 1975 pizza oven that combines its power with awesome ancestral recipes. Making a pizza that tastes so good that my sisters from other misters, Debi and Cindy, will drive all the way from Howe, Indiana to eat it. They say, "It's worth the 2-hour one-way trip!"

According to an interview given by grandson, Dany Zunica, it was his grandfather, Dante Zunica, who first opened House of Pizza in 1954, and in the very spot it still operates to this day. "We are still in the original building," Zunica stated, "...we've never moved."

Growing over six decades, this business has now expanded into what was originally six different storefronts in order to accommodate their ever-growing clientele.

"Today we have a full bar with a lounge, a family dining area, a room for parties, and the menu has expanded as well," he said.

The one thing that continues to set House of Pizza apart from other pizza parlors is their commitment to serving fresh food from "Old Country" recipes.

"All of our food is made fresh in-house," Zunica said. "Customers love the homemade cheese-cake, which was my great grandma's recipe, but what we are really known for is our thin-crust pizza. We make our own dough and our own sauce, and even the sausage, which was my grandma's recipe, too! Another thing that sets us apart is that we 've been using the same pizza oven since 1975, and that affects how the pizza cooks. This is why our pizza still has the same great taste as it did when you were a kid," making House of Pizza a true asset that continues to provide us with old-fashioned-fabulous food!

GIOVANNI'S (1966-present) began with a struggling restaurant that Italian immigrant, Procopio LoDuca, decided to buy to open his own pizzeria. By 1976, with the help of his wife Nancy, his wager was paying off so well that they were able to double the building's size and create an exceptional Italian dining restaurant that would go on to earn national acclaim.

Known for its excellent food, ambiance, and service, you never walk out of here without a smile on your face. In fact, my husband enjoyed their artichoke hearts in creamed spinach appetizer so much that I had to develop a recipe to create it for him at home!

[FYI: My recipe for it appears just a bit later in this book!]

We loved dinners at Giovanni's. The fresh rolls and bread served with a trio of butter, oil and spices. The fresh parmesan cheese and the amazing appetizers and entrees, and of course the tiramisu and cannoli with their great coffee or tea.

As family members passed on, the family made the decision to sell to new owners in October of 2020. Thus, ending the family's fifty-four-year highly-successful run, but also enabling Giovanni's doors to remain open to the Calumet Region so we can continue to enjoy this favorite gem!

ZEL'S (1965-present) is where I turn when I get a hankering for an Andes hot beef! Opening its first location in the spring of 1965, when Stanley and Faye Routman opened a small yellow building at the corner of Columbus Drive and Euclid Avenue in the Indiana Harbor section of East Chicago, they honorably named their restaurant after a family member.

With more locations being added, the Hammond location on 169th Street (that I have often popped into), has been in operation since 1983.

As someone who knows that a restaurant is only as good as its employees and the product it sells, it speaks volumes that the level of quality in the products they provide have not changed in all the years they have been in business, and it also says something about the management that 10 percent of ZEL'S work force has been on the job more than thirty years!

In 1998, the Routmans sold their interest in all the ZEL'S locations and local real estate broker, Robert Shah (with his daughter and son-in-law), Luke Oil businessmen, Tom Collins, and Hobart businessman, Don Jelnik, decided to make the purchase.

"We still use only 100 percent USDA choice beef. And it's a two-day process to prepare it for our sandwiches," stated Bob Shah in an interview. "We have not changed our preparation method or the quality of our food. Why fix it if it's not broke?" Thanks to the sale, ZEL'S still offers four locations in the Calumet Region: East Chicago, Hammond, Crown Point and Schererville. I love that we still get to enjoy the slow-cooked flavor of an oh-my-goodness-good Italian beef sandwich!

MINER DUNN (1932-present) is where you go for an old-fashioned burger (and more) served the old-fashioned way. Offering the same fresh-made burgers topped with creamy Old English cheese (the way they have all these years) you also still get that pile of fresh-cut fries or freshly sliced and battered onion rings, and a serving of signature orange sherbet that's brought to you by servers who have worked there for decades!

With corned beef and roast beef cooked and sliced in-house for Reuben and French dips, and meatloaf touted to be as good as your mother's, it's hard to make room for their homemade vegetable soup and homemade pies, but remarkably most people do!

CAVALIER INN (1949-present) is where you go when you want to sink your fork into old-fashioned Eastern European Polish food made right!

Proud of their Polish heritage, this restaurant has been family-owned and operated from the very start. This family's commitment is to serve the Calumet Region, and their service motto is to treat every customer like they were a part of their family.

Their amazing, true-to-Polish food that's made-to-order no less is what I like to call, "old country" home-style polish food, and includes items such as potato pancakes that are full-bodied, and cabbage rolls that taste just like Mom used to make! Its the kind of place that's a 'must' for returning region natives to go!

BLUE TOP (1938-present) helps you conjure up the "Happy Days" feeling that many equate with the 1950's drive-in craze, but the Blue Top in Highland actually got its start more than a decade sooner. With simple beginnings as a fruit stand opened by Copenhagen, Denmark immigrant, William Louis Johnsen.

The owner of a filling station on Indianapolis Boulevard in Highland, Johnsen thought to cash in on the tourist trade that paraded through Wicker Park, so he put up food stands to serve the motorists specializing in selling apple cider, peanuts, and fruit.

Leaving his two sons to run the operation while he and his wife, Julia (nee Cieniawski) went on vacation, and one of the instructions they left with the boys was to "Fix up the stands." The boys struck a bargain with a local, George Fishtorn, who owned the lumber company.

Their deal was to trade lumber, materials, and workers for gas in the lumber yard's trucks, which enabled the boys to expand the stand to a building about half the size of a garage at the filling station.

Doing this without their father knowing, the boys had the farm stand built to be triple the size of what their father wanted. In a few weeks' time the building was done, and since the shingled roof was blue, they named it the "Blue Top!"

As time marched forward the business expanded, and would close during winter months until 1964, when the new Blue Top Drive-in was built.

Offering a special ambiance that it still exudes to this day, the Blue Top is a true beauty and as a result draws from all walks of life, including some famous notables such as boxer Joe Louis, the Chicago Bears (on their way to summer training camp in southern Indiana), and even Katherine Hepburn, who stopped there on her way to Florida.

TEIBEL'S (1929-present) has provided the Calumet Region area with over ninety-three years of delicious dining service!

Opening its doors as a simple, 12-seat highway diner, brothers Martin and Stephen Teibel opened on the corner of Routes 30 and Highway 41 with no idea how quickly word would spread about their delicious homemade fried chicken and their freshly-made sandwiches.

Over the years there have been some changes, such as expanding from their original 12 seats to having the ability to comfortably accommodate up to 600, but many things have remained unchanged.

Such as the Teibel family's commitment to superior service and quality food, which they pair with the same recipes that the Teibel family brought over from Austria (Maybe we're related!) and why people still yearn for the unmistakable flavor of their famous perch.

At Teibel's they say customers can always count on two things: Your meal will taste as good as it always has, and their friendly and efficient staff will make you feel right at home!

A few other Calumet Region area restaurants that have managed to endure the test of time, and stick to the old classic menus we came to know and love from the 50s, 60s and 70s, make them definitely worth mentioning.

The Schererville Lounge and Restaurant (1980s-present) in Schererville is still being touted for its old-fashioned bread basket with breadsticks and cheese, dinners that still come with relish trays featuring beets and coleslaw. Loaves of bread that get served with honey butter. Soup or salad and a potato, and lake perch, and other entrees they cook to perfection. Known in more recent times for their AYCE crab legs, if you like that "old school" dining atmosphere and service, then Schererville Lounge is a place that is perfect for you!

Freddy's Steak House (1965-present) in Hessville, has served the Calumet region for the past fifty-seven years. First established by the Matson Family, who built its reputation as a place for spectacular steaks and seafood, the restaurant was sold to the Kamradt Family in 2015, who is proud to continue using many of the original recipes and traditions that have been in place since the original owners. These include offering you a choice of a side and a choice of soup or salad, as well as the complimentary fresh-baked bread that comes warm from the oven!

The Town Club Restaurant (1947-present) in Highland shows its age in a good way, by exuding a comforting "old school" vibe, offering the biggest and best martini in the Region, and a classic menu that offers multiple fresh fish choices, prime rib, seafood, and even frog legs! Their ambiance, menu selections, service and special flavors combine to create that magical feel of yester-year that customers get to eat up one bite at a time!

El Taco Real (1974-present) in north Hammond first opened its doors because husband and owner, Raymundo Alcorta Garcia thought that his wife, Esther Anguiano Garcia, cooked so good that it should be served in a restaurant.

Run by family in what is now its forty-eighth year of business, El Taco Real credits its success to its great customers that enjoy being treated like family, and eating delicious food served in family-sized portions.

El Taco Real continues to do their own hand-trimming of meat, hand-cutting lettuce and tomatoes, and cooking everything from scratch. It's no wonder why they have been crowned "Best of the Region" in Mexican food for many, many years!

Chuck & Irene's (1947-present) in Hammond first opened an East Chicago location. Charles "Chuck" and Irene Basso eventually opened and a second, **Chuck & Irene's** in Hammond then down-sized to just the Hammond location.

In operation for an impressive seventy-five years, Chuck & Irene's continues to be run by Chuck and Irene's son, Anthony, "Tony" Basso, and his wife, Geri, and their son, Tony.
Attaining the status of being the oldest established business in Hessville, their longevity is a testament to how appreciated quality food and service at economical prices truly are.

Offering a simple, no nonsense, tavern-lost-in-time atmosphere, Chuck & Irene's still offers unheard of weekend specials that include all-you-can-eat ocean perch, catfish, walleye, breaded shrimp, breaded scallops, smelt, and more. Weeknight specials vary, but usually include bottomless baskets of popcorn shrimp and smelt!

MADVEK'S (1972-present) in Hammond is the only place in the Calumet Region (that I know of) that still serves the legendary loose meat, Maid Rite-style sandwiches!

A definite, "old school" style hot dog stand complete with a standing-room-only lunch counter, Madvek's was first opened by George and Violet Madvek, who served up snappy red hots and savory loose meat hamburgers 13 hours a day, every day, making their restaurant a Calumet Region institution.

With George Madvek passing on in 1990, Violet eventually sold Madvek's in 1996 to longtime customers, Richard and Mary White, who also happen to own Dick's Body Shop next door. "When we bought the restaurant," Mary White stated, "Mrs. Madvek (Violet) stayed with me for that first month. She taught me everything about the food."

In 2008, Violet went to be with George, and thanks to the White's great service to the community their legacy and their delicious recipes live on at this very special diner. In 2010, the City of Hammond bestowed an honor to George and Violet's legacy by renaming a portion of 169th Place (outside the restaurant) "Madvek's Place."

In 2012, Madvek's had the esteemed honor (and pleasure) of being featured on Chicago's entertainment and foodie television program, 190 North, which threw a spotlight on them for being a rare diner that still serves up good old-fashioned quality food, especially those old-school Maid Rite-style sandwiches, and high quality service!

Growing up in an environment that offers so many delicious food choices has its ups and downs. The "up" is that you get to experience and indulge yourself in all these wonderful foods. The "down" is that you are spoiled by them and the Calumet Region dishes become a stick by which all other food are measured against.

Life has taught me (after clocking sixty-one trips around the sun) that the unique melting pot of flavors that we are so blessed to have in the Calumet Region is truly special, absolutely delight-ful, and unique. Despite all the much-loved places closing down, and me moving around, the desire for Calumet Region cuisine continues to following me like an old ghost! Haunting me to the point where I had to do something to satisfy the cravings that memories of it bring.

In an attempt to satisfy these highly-spirited cravings, here now are some of my favorite recipes that were inspired by the incredible and oh-so-unforgettable Calumet Region cuisine!

Laura's Calumet Region-inspired Sweet 'n' Sour Slaw

Yield: 8 servings
1 cup white sugar
1 cup vinegar
2 teaspoons celery seeds
1/2 cup light vegetable oil
1 medium cabbage, shredded
1 green pepper, chopped
1 carrot, chopped
1 onion, chopped
In a small saucepan, combine, vinegar, celery seeds, and oil. Bring to a boil, reduce to a simmer and cook for 5 minutes. Pour over vegetables, salt to taste, then chill overnight before serving.~

Laura's Condes Deli-inspired Cool 'n' Creamy Slaw

Yield: 8 servings
8 cups finely diced cabbage (about 1 head)
1/4 cup diced carrot
2 tablespoons minced onion
1/2 green bell pepper, seeded and minced
1/3 cup granulated sugar
1/2 teaspoon salt
1/2 teaspoon pepper
1 teaspoon celery seeds
1/2 cup sour cream
1/2 cup mayonnaise
1 tablespoon grated horseradish
1 tablespoon white vinegar
1 tablespoon lemon juice
Dice cabbage and carrots, fine. Pour cabbage and carrots into a large bowl and stir in minced onions. Using regular blade on food processor, process remaining ingredients until smooth. Pour over vegetable mixture and mix thoroughly. Cover bowl and refrigerate several hours or overnight before serving.

Calumet Region-inspired Classic Three Bean Salad

Yield: 8 servings
1 (15 1/2 ounce) can red kidney beans
1 (15 1/2 ounce) can yellow wax beans
1 (15 1/2 ounce) can green beans
1/2 cup diced celery
3 tablespoons sweet pickle relish
4 green onions, chopped
1/4 teaspoon salt, or to taste
Fresh ground black pepper
1/3 cup olive oil (or salad oil)
2/3 cup vinegar
Red onion rings, chopped green onion, or green bell pepper rings for garnish. Combine all the ingredients except the garnish and toss lightly.
Chill well. Present in a chilled bowl and with desired garnish.

⊠alumet ⊠egion-inspired ⊠lassic ⊠idney ⊠ean Salad

Yield: 6 servings
1/4 cup sweet pickle relish
3/4 cup (or more) favorite style mayonnaise
1 sweet onion, minced
6 inner, celery heart stalks, diced
30 ounces canned red kidney beans, rinsed and drained
2 hard-boiled eggs, peeled, and chopped
salt and pepper, to taste

In a serving bowl, bowl, combine relish and mayonnaise with onion and celery, mixing well. Add kidney beans then salt and pepper, and stir well, then fold in chopped boiled egg and gently blend in. Chill at least 4 hours in the refrigerator then taste to adjust seasoning, if desired, before serving.

Calumet Region and Phil Smidt-inspired Classics: Frog Legs, Boned and Buttered Perch and the Classic Fish Fry

Calumet Region-inspired Fish Fry

Yield: 4 servings

1 sleeve saltine crackers, finely ground
1 tablespoon cornmeal (optional)
1 teaspoon finely-ground black pepper
1/4 teaspoon cayenne pepper
1/2 teaspoon sweet paprika
8 ounces fresh lake fish fillets
butter, for frying
fresh lemon, for squeezing over cooked fish (optional)

In a plastic or paper bag, combine ground crackers with cornmeal (if using), black pepper, and cayenne powder. Close bag and shake to mix well.

Add fish then close bag and toss to coat all sides, then set aside. In a skillet over medium heat, add butter and melt. Working in batches, place coated fish into skillet, skin side down, and cook just until the sides of fish start to curl up, about 2 minutes.

Carefully turn fish over to cook other side for about 1 minute then transfer cooked fish to a warm serving plate.

Squeeze fresh lemon juice over the top just before serving (if using).

[Alternate Method: I take two sleeves of unsalted saltines and one box of Drakes seasoning and blend in a food processor until a finely milled. I then place it in an airtight plastic bag and use it to bread fish, chicken, or shrimp, placing any unused into freezer to keep fresh and ready for me.] ~

1869-inspired Great Lakes Tartar Sauce

1 egg yolk (pasteurized)
1 cup sweet-oil (olive)
1 tablespoonful of dry mustard
3 shallots, minced
6 gherkins, minced
1 tablespoonful of parsley, minced
1 small pinch of Cayenne pepper

Place egg yolk in a whisking bowl then, using a whisk, beat yolk while slowly drizzling oil in. Whisk in remaining ingredients and chill until serving.~

Phil Smidt-inspired Boned and Buttered Perch

2 tablespoons oil
1 1/2 pounds small as you can get, skinless perch fillets, cut into 4-inch pieces
1 tablespoon fresh chopped Italian parsley
4 tablespoons unsalted butter
1 tablespoon lemon juice

In a large skillet, heat oil until shimmering. Add half of the fillets into the skillet and sauté over moderately high heat until lightly browned and cooked through, about 3-4 minutes per side. Transfer fish to a warmed platter and repeat with the remaining fillets. Season with salt and pepper and sprinkle with the parsley; hold warm. Into same skillet, melt butter, add lemon juice, swirling skillet to blend, then pour sauce over fish and serve. ~

Phil Smidt-inspired Frog Legs

1-1/4 cups all-purpose flour
2 tablespoons potato starch (preferably) or corn starch
1-1/2 teaspoons seasoned salt
2 pounds frog's legs, smallest you can get
Butter-flavored cooking oil, for frying

In an electric skillet preferably, or a Dutch oven fitted with a thermometer, bring about an inches-worth of butter-flavored oil up to 375 degrees, then adjust heat to maintain it (and why I recommend an electric skillet). In a plastic or paper bag, combine the flour with the starch and seasoned salt, then shake the bag to blend ingredients together well. Add frog legs to bag, then close bag and shake and pat it to coat the legs well. Add a few legs, do not over-crowd, to 375-degree oil and fry for 3 minutes, then turn over and continue to fry until crisp and brown, about 3 more minutes. Serve with Frog Sauce (on next page) if desired.~

Phil Smidt-inspired Frog Leg (tartar) Sauce

1/2 bunch Italian flat-leaf parsley, stems removed
1/2 cup sweet pickles
1 small sweet onion
1 cup mayonnaise

In the bowl of a blender or processor, combine all ingredients then blend until just slightly chunky. Remove to a storage container and refrigerate until use, storing un-used portion in an airtight container in fridge for up to 3 days. ~

Phil Smidt-inspired Kidney Bean Relish Salad

Yield: 4 servings

1 (15 ounce) can kidney beans, drained and rinsed
1/2 cup diced celery hearts
1/4 cup diced sweet pickles
1 small sweet onion, juiced*
1/2 cup distilled white vinegar
2 tablespoons granulated sugar
1/2 teaspoon salt

*= The easiest way to juice an onion is to run through a blender or a food processor then strain, pressing on solids, to release all the juice possible.

In a medium bowl, combine all ingredient, stir well, then cover and refrigerate for at least 8 hours or overnight before serving so that flavors have the chance to develop and penetrate the beans. ~

Calumet Region-inspired Fried Shrimp

Yield: 6 servings

light oil for frying

16 ounces large raw shrimp, peeled and de-veined

1 sleeve unsalted saltine crackers

1/2 cup cornmeal

1/2 cup all-purpose flour

1/4 cup potato starch (preferably) or corn starch

2 large eggs

1/4 cup buttermilk (or milk with 1/2 teaspoon of white vinegar added to it)

In an electric skillet preferably, or a Dutch oven fitted with a thermometer, bring about one inch worth of light oil up to 365 degrees, then adjust heat to maintain it (this is why I recommend an electric skillet). Line a large plate with a paper towel, set aside, then rinse shrimp well and leave to drain.

In the bowl of a blender or food processor, combine saltines with cornmeal and salt then blend/process until the mixture is the consistency of cornmeal. Pour into a cake or pie pan and set aside.

In a second cake or pie pan, whisk eggs together with buttermilk (or milk) and set aside.

In a third cake or pie pan, combine the cornstarch and flour.

On a work surface, line up pans so that cornstarch and flour are first, egg second and cornmeal/cracker mix is last in line. Place prepped shrimp in the cornstarch/flour mixture, tossing to coat. Shake odd excess then transfer shrimp to the egg mixture, turning to coat well. Then transfer shrimp to the cornmeal cracker crumb mixture, pressing in to coat well.

Place breaded shrimp on a clean plate, then repeat steps with all remaining shrimp.

Once all shrimp are ready (they can be frozen for future cooking or) begin adding them to preheated oil, being careful not to overcrowd. Fry for about 3 minutes, or until crispy and golden brown. Drain on prepared plate. Repeat with remaining shrimp. ~

Freddy's-inspired Shrimp Cocktail

Yield: 4 servings.

1/2 cup white vinegar
1/2 cup water
1 tablespoon Old Bay Seasoning
1 tablespoon pickling spice
1 bay leaf
1 clove
3 peppercorns
1 lemon, sliced
1 pound shrimp, raw large thawed (shell-on produces more flavor)

In a large saucepan, combine vinegar, water, seasonings, and lemon. Over high heat, bring mixture to a rolling boil then reduce to a simmer and cook, covered, for 10 minutes.

Remove lid from pan, add shrimp, cover, and remove pan from heat. Allow the pan to rest, covered, without disturbing for 3 minutes. Stir shrimp then check for doneness. Shrimp should have turned from opaque to white and feel plumped up and firm.

Let shrimp rest in the hot bath in the pan until all shrimp are cooked through, then move shrimp to a strainer and rinse gently to remove cooking debris before plating. Serve immediately with sauce and lemon wedges.

NOTE: If serving chilled, plunge shrimp into an ice water bath for 5 minutes before serving. ~

Super-Quick Shrimp Cocktail Sauce

Yield: 4 servings.

1 cup ketchup
2 tablespoons grated horseradish (to taste)
1 tablespoon lemon juice
1/2 teaspoon Worcestershire sauce (optional)

Mix all ingredients and chill until use. ~

Vogel's-inspired Shrimp De Jonghe

Yield: 4 servings.

12 tablespoons unsalted butter (1 1/2 sticks)
1 teaspoon natural fine mineral sea salt
1 to 2 cloves garlic, finely minced (or more, to taste)
1 cup finely-ground saltines or Italian bread
1/3 cup minced parsley
1/2 cup dry sherry
Dash of cayenne pepper
Dash of sweet paprika
2 pounds large raw shrimp

Preheat oven to 375 degrees. In a mixer or bowl, cream together butter, salt, and garlic. Mix in breadcrumbs, parsley, sherry, pepper and paprika.

[Alternately, place everything but the shrimp into a food processor and pulse until blended well.]

Peel, devein, rinse, and drain shrimp on a towel and set aside.

Butter 4 to 6 individual, ovenproof casserole dishes (or one 9 x 12" dish).

Sprinkle a little of the breadcrumb mixture into the bottom of the dishes, then divide shrimp among the dishes.

Sprinkle remaining breadcrumb mixture over the top of all the dishes then place in oven.

Bake until crumbs are golden brown and sizzling, and shrimp cooks through, about 20-25 minutes.

Remove from oven and let rest 5 minutes before serving. ~

Giovanni's-inspired Fried Artichoke Hearts in a Spinach Cream Sauce

Yield: 4 servings.

1 (14-15 ounce) can baby (or smallest you can find) artichoke hearts, drained
1 egg, beaten
1 tablespoon water
1 tablespoon grated Parmesan cheese
flour for coating
breadcrumbs, for coating
dried thyme
dried parsley
oil for deep frying
10 ounces frozen spinach, thawed and drained
3 tablespoons unsalted butter
2 tablespoons all-purpose flour
1 cup of half & half, milk, or cream
4 ounces Neufchatel cheese
1/2 cup grated Parmesan
1 teaspoon garlic powder
1/2 teaspoon black pepper
Dash cayenne powder

Drain artichoke hearts, gently squeezing out any water in them. Move to a cut-ting board and carefully cut the artichokes in half, and then in half again (if desired) to form quarters. Set aside. Beat egg with water then add Parmesan and salt and pepper and pour into a small bowl. In a low-rimmed bowl, place some flour, and in a third, low-rimmed bowl, place some breadcrumbs. To breadcrumbs add a sprinkle of parsley, thyme, salt and pepper. Line up bowls beginning with flour, then egg, then breadcrumbs. Dip artichoke quarters first into flour then egg, then breadcrumbs, coating all sides well with each ingredient. Set breaded artichokes on a plate. Once all are coated, in a deep fry pan, heat oil, and when hot, begin frying breaded artichoke hearts, turning as they brown on both sides, about 3-5 minutes per side, to desired doneness. Remove browned hearts to a warm, paper towel-lined plate. Hold warm. Once all hearts have been browned, drain any remaining oil from pan and return to stove. In pan, using a whisk or similar utensil, whisk together flour and butter until flour is completely absorbed by butter then add Neufchatel and whisk to incorporate. Slowly pour in half & half, blending together well. Add spinach, blend ingredients, then place pan over medium heat. Stir continually, bring to a boil then add Parmesan, garlic powder and peppers. Stir, cooking until cheese melts then remove from heat. Pour sauce onto a shallow, lipped, oven-proof serving dish then arrange artichokes over the sauce. Sprinkle with a garnish of additional Parmesan, if desired, salt and pepper to taste, then run under a broiler to crisp and brown slightly before serving. ~

Andes-inspired Crockpot Italian Beef Sandwiches (with or without the peppers!)

Yield: 8 to 10 servings

1 large sweet onion, minced (optional)
1 (16 ounce) jar giardiniera peppers, mild or hot (optional)
4 to 5 pounds beef chuck roast
1 tablespoon coarsely-ground black pepper
1 tablespoon dried marjoram (Greek Oregano)
1 tablespoon onion powder
1 tablespoon quality garlic powder
1 tablespoon dried basil
1 bay leaf
1 dry package of Good Seasons Italian salad dressing mix
1 quart low-sodium beef broth

Chop onion and place in the bottom of a crock pot. Add giardiniera (if using), then place roast on top of the vegetables and begin sprinkling meat with black pepper then, marjoram (Greek Oregano), onion powder, garlic powder, basil, bay leaf, and package of Good Seasons Italian salad dressing mix. Pour the quart of low-sodium chicken broth over the roast to help spread the seasonings around, then cover and cook according to your preferred time schedule. Turn crock pot to "high" to cook for 4 hours, or to"low" to cook for 8 hours or overnight. Once meat has cooked, remove it to a cutting board. Returning to crock pot, inspect the juice and remove any bones, gristle, and bay leaf. Returning to roast, remove any bones and gristle then, using two forks, shred meat then place it in the inspected juice. Once all meat is in juice, let it cook on low for at least 15 minutes before serving.

Great served on Turano-type rolls, especially when dipped in that amazing au jus (meat juice), of course!

House of Pizza-inspired Neapolitan Pizza

Yield: two 12-inch pizzas
1 teaspoon granulated sugar
1 cup warm water, 105 degrees
1/2 package active dry yeast
2 1/2 cups unbleached flour
1/2 teaspoon salt
1 tablespoon fresh basil
1 teaspoon fresh Greek oregano (marjoram)
Pastorelli brand pizza sauce (or favorite)
fresh tomatoes (optional)
1/2-pound shredded provolone cheese
1/2-pound shredded mozzarella cheese
1/2-pound sweet Italian sausage or your favorite toppings
1/4 cup grated parmesan cheese

In a large, warm mixing bowl, mix sugar into the warm water. Sprinkle yeast on top. Wait for 10 minutes or until yeast starts moving. Add flour and salt, then mix by hand until combined. Cover loosely and let rest at room temperature for 4 hours then place in refrigerator overnight or up to 3 days before you need to use. When ready to use, preheat oven to 425 degrees. Lightly grease two 12-inch pizza pans. Then divide dough in half.

Heavily flour a rolling surface then, using a rolling pin, roll each dough half into a 14-inch circle. then transfer to prepared pans. Place in preheated oven and bake for 7 to 10 minutes. Remove from oven, spread crusts with pizza sauce and then sprinkle with fresh basil,Greek oregano (marjoram), and cheese. Add any toppings you like, keeping center of pizza less crowded with toppings than the outer circle area, so that it cooks evenly.

Return pizza to oven and Bake for 10-20 minutes, depending on toppings, or until bubbly and toppings are fully cooked as desired. Remove pizza from oven and sprinkle with parmesan before slicing and serving.

Anyone from the Calumet Region knows the flavor of a good pizza, and anyone who has left the area knows how unique it is as well. This conundrum led me to develop a recipe to satisfy cravings whenever and wherever I am. Like horseshoes, it comes close.
The key is to age the dough, use Greek oregano (marjoram) and Chicago brand Pastorelli sauce, which is available at Meijer (even in Michigan!)

The rich blend of ethnicities that the Calumet Region offered to me in my youth had a huge impact on my palate, and to be honest, influences my cooking to this day. In fact, it was such a strong influencer that it motivated me to create the riffs on the old restaurant menu items I just mentioned, and it's also caused me to attempt my own renditions of longtime community favorites as well, like eclairs and the unforgettable paczki!

From the Boulevard Bakery to Almira's, and various other bakeries and donut shops in between, one could not grow up in the Calumet Region without experiencing the joy of sinking your teeth into freshly-made, cream-filled donuts, eclairs and cream puffs all year round. Plus, the added excitement of enjoying paczki, which were made especially for consumption on Fat Tuesday. To recapture the old-fashioned "just-made" fresh taste from yesteryear, try making some at home.

Paczkis Pronto

2 cans (10-count) refrigerated biscuits

Vegetable shortening for frying

In a Dutch oven, heat 1 inch of shortening to 365 degrees. Carefully separate biscuits, and then drop in hot shortening until brown, about 45 seconds. With a slotted spoon, turn donuts over and fry until brown on the other side. Remove to drain on a brown paper bag. ~

Bavarian Cream Paczki Filling
1 package French Vanilla Instant Pudding
1 cup milk
1 cup Half & Half
GLAZE
2 cups powdered sugar
1/4 cup un-sweetened cocoa powder
1 teaspoon pure vanilla extract
1/4 cup milk
Make pudding according to package directions using 1 cup milk and 1 cup Half & Half. Place pudding into a pastry tube or a condiment squeeze bottle with a pointed spout. Using tip, pierce side of donut then wiggle the tip around to create a space for the pudding.
Squeeze container to fill donut. Stop when pudding begins ooze out of hole. Repeat with remaining donuts. To make GLAZE: In a small bowl, stir together powdered sugar, cocoa and vanilla then add milk until desired consistency is reached- about 1/4 cup. Dip one side of donut into glaze then place on serving plate. ~

Jelly-filled Paczki Filling
2 cups of your favorite jelly
GLAZE
2 cups powdered sugar
Place jelly into a pastry tube or a condiment squeeze bottle with a pointed spout. Using tip, pierce side of donut then wiggle tip around to create a space for jelly. Squeeze container to fill donut. Stop when jelly begins to ooze out of hole. Repeat with remaining donuts.
GLAZE: In a small bowl, place powdered sugar. Roll filled donut in sugar then place on a serving plate. ~

Luscious Lemon Paczki Filling

1 package Lemon Instant Pudding
1 cup milk
1 cup Half & Half
GLAZE
2 cups powdered sugar
1 teaspoon pure lemon extract
1/4 cup milk

Make pudding according to package directions using 1 cup milk and 1 cup Half & Half. Place pudding into a pastry tube or a condiment squeeze bottle with a pointed spout. Using tip, pierce side of donut then wiggle the tip around to create a space for the pudding. Squeeze container to fill donut. Stop when pudding begins ooze out of hole. Repeat with remaining donuts.

GLAZE: In a small bowl, stir together powdered sugar and lemon extract then add milk until you reach desired consistency- about 1/4 cup. Dip one side of donut into glaze then place on serving plate. ~

Classic Cream Puffs

1 cup water
1/4 teaspoon salt
4 eggs
3 tablespoons powdered sugar
6 tablespoons baking cocoa
1 cup confectioners' sugar
2 tablespoons hot water
1/2 cup butter
1 cup all-purpose flour
1 cup heavy cream, cold
3/4 teaspoon pure vanilla extract
5 tablespoons butter
1 teaspoon vanilla extract

Preheat oven to 400 degrees. In saucepan, bring water, butter, and salt to a boil. Add flour all at once and stir until it forms a ball. Remove from heat, let stand 5 minutes. Add eggs, one at a time, beating well after each addition and until the mixture is smooth and not shiny.

Drop by 1/4 cups onto a greased baking sheet. Bake for 30-35 minutes or until lightly golden brown. Remove to a wire rack and let cool. To make filling: in the bowl of a stand mixer with whisk attachment in place, whip cream until it just starts to thicken. Add sugar and vanilla, continue whipping until soft to medium peaks form. Fill a pastry bag with the cream, and pipe into the bottom of the puffs until filled. To make glaze: in a small, heavy saucepan, melt cocoa and butter together over low heat, about 5 minutes. Remove from heat and stir in confectioners' sugar and vanilla extract.

Stir in hot water, 1 teaspoon at a time, until glaze is thick and smooth. Drizzle over cream puffs . Yield: 8 servings~

After being anointed an honorary Buscia, and being accompanied by my "helpers" that day, which included with my lovely daughter and absolutely adorable granddaughters, who were thrilled to be flanked by the oh-so-awesome 2018 Pierogi Fest Buscias (left to right) Dru Revis, Theresa Meyer, Laine Kaminsky, and Carolyn Krusz. God bless the Buscias, especially Chamber Executive Director, Diane Kaminsky (left photo), who helped make this oh-so-precious moment possible!

Growing up on pierogi, in the "little city by the lake" and having them made fresh everywhere all the time, I never thought much about them until I moved and couldn't find them. This drove me to learn how to make them and teach the grandkids so the tradition could be passed down.

Dear, departed sister Nancy excelled at pierogi-making. Hers were the best and it became one of her many facets that I will always cherish and miss.

Pierogi-making is so easy that some consider it child's play.

Personally, I think it's a good idea to get the kids involved because you can never have enough extra hands in the kitchen to do these small tasks, and it can become a teachable moment, too.

A golden opportunity to pass down a special, ancestral recipe to your own next of kin in the process.

The bonus is everyone gets to eat their fill of these oh-so-delicious pierogi!

Calumet Region-inspired Potato-Cheddar Pierogi

6 large eggs
6 cups all-purpose flour, plus more for dusting
1 cup mashed potatoes -no lumps/ skins
1 teaspoon baking powder
1 teaspoon salt
1/2 cup water
FILLING
2 1/2 pounds Idaho russet potatoes
1 tablespoon sweet Hungarian paprika
2 teaspoons garlic powder
2 teaspoons onion powder
1 tablespoon salt
2 teaspoons freshly ground black pepper
8 ounces Cheddar, shredded
4 ounces cream cheese
all-purpose flour, for dusting

In the bowl of a stand mixer fitted with the dough hook attachment, add eggs, flour, mashed potatoes, baking powder, salt and 1/2 cup water. Mix until the dough is smooth and elastic, about 5 minutes. Cover the dough in plastic wrap or a slightly damp cloth. Let rest in the refrigerator for at least 15 minutes and up to 4 hours before using.

For Filling: Put the potatoes in a medium pot and cover with cold water. Bring to a boil and cook until fork tender, 20 to 30 minutes. Drain the potatoes and let rest until the skins are dry. Transfer the potatoes to a mixing bowl, removing skins. Mash potatoes until just broken up. Add paprika, garlic powder, onion powder, salt and pepper. Continue mashing until there are no lumps and the dry ingredients are thoroughly mixed in. Add cream cheese and continue mixing until blended. Add Cheddar; mix until blended. Refrigerate until chilled.

To assemble: Bring a large pot of water to a boil. Meanwhile, on a well-floured surface, roll out a ball of Pierogi Dough the size of a large orange into a rectangle about 1/8-inch thick. Cut out 3-inch rounds of dough (a pint glass will do). Place 2 tablespoons of filling in the center of each round, then fold the rounds in half. Make sure all air pockets are pressed out of pierogi. Crimp the edges with a fork or your fingers. Place completed pierogi in boiling water for 3 minutes, or until they float. Using a slotted spoon, remove pierogi to a wire rack to drain. At this point, pierogi can be frozen in single layers or browned in butter in a skillet.

To cook Frozen Pierogi: Bring pot of water to boil. Place frozen pierogi into water and cook until they float. Using a slotted spoon, remove pierogi to a wire rack to drain. Heat a skillet with butter and then add pierogi, turning to brown and crisp all sides, to desired doneness. Yield: 50 ~

My oldest friend, Cary, has been a "sister from another mister" since 1975, when we met the very first day of high school. She and I were seated one in front of the other in French class. When French class ended, we discovered that we were also in Algebra together. Then we discovered we shared the same lunch hour, and then shared the same gym class, so clearly the universe wanted the two of us to come together.

We shared lots of common things, like both coming from private catholic grade schools, both having similar Eastern European backgrounds. We formed an instant bond because we both were in the process of transitioning from a more cloistered, private catholic school life of uniforms and nuns to a public high school life that felt more like a free-for-all in comparison.

Cary's parents, Paul and Kay, made me feel almost instantly part of their family and have kept that closeness with me up and to this day. While there have been many a recipe convo between us in what now spans more than forty-seven years, there is one recipe that always comes to mind when I think of them, likely because it was so different than anything Mom ever made, and that was Kay's Grasshopper Pie.

Learning about it one afternoon while sitting in their kitchen, as Kay was pulling it out of the freezer, I saw something oddly green and had to ask. She explained that it was a freezer pie inspired by a 1950s chocolate-mint cocktail called the Grasshopper. Using a special recipe that combined ice cream with whipped cream and a splash of crème de menthe, this pie is served frozen then sprinkled with dark chocolate, so it's no wonder it became an unforgettable memory for me.

Originally made with cookies or graham cracker crumb crust, Kay made her pie using Oreo cookies that she had Cary separate, scrape the cream centers out, then crush. It gave both the crust and the pie a far more distinctive flavor, which in turn made it unforgettable for me.

A lifelong Whiting-Robertsdale resident, and a "sister from another mister" since 1975, Cary and I have shared school dances, celebrated our 50 trips around the sun at Tommy Gun's (in 2011), and have fun together with food, in various ways, in more recent times. My, how 47 years just flies by!

Knowing Cary since 1975, her entire family has come to make me feel welcome in their lives, hearts, and home. Cary's mom, Kay, along-with Cary and her sons, Niko, (Demitri not pictured), and Ian are accompanied by Cary's dad and Kay's loving husband, Paul, to witness Ian being sworn in as one of Whiting's finest at Whiting City Hall. God bless them all!

Kay's Fabulous Frozen Grasshopper Pie
1 pint mint chocolate chip ice cream
8 ounces frozen non-dairy whipped topping, thawed
1 ounce Cream de Menthe liquor
1 Oreo piecrust
Garnish (optional): Chocolate chips or shavings
Remove ice cream from freezer and let stand at room temperature for 15 minutes.
In the large bowl of an electric mixer, using the whisk attachment, blend ice cream until smooth.
Add whipped topping then the liquor.
Pour filling into piecrust and cover with plastic wrap.
Place in freezer on a level surface and freeze for 6 hours or until firm.
Place pie in refrigerator 30 minutes before serving to soften.
Garnish (optional) with chocolate chips or shavings. ~

A fellow, "sister from another mister," Lorraine (Lori as I call her) met through a mutual friend back in 1979. A Catholic girl from north Hammond, Lori is so positive and friendly that you can't not be friends with her.

She is someone that is hard to say, "No!" to. As such, she got me to join a local volleyball team with her when we were just out of high school.

Lori's deep spiritual beliefs helped me to learn to shift my thoughts away from negativity and instead focus on the brighter side of life. This mindset greatly aided me in getting through those dark, early days after my father's sudden death, and I am eternally grateful to her for helping me get through all that.

I count myself very fortunate that time and tide have not caused our friendship to drift apart, and I feel honored to have such a peaceful and God-loving person that I get to call my friend.

Lori's Mom's City Chicken

1.5 pounds city chicken (pork or veal pieces cut into cubes)
salt and pepper
2 eggs
1 cup seasoned bread crumbs
1/2 teaspoon paprika
2 tablespoons Parmesan cheese
1/2 cup vegetable oil
1/2 cup chicken stock, broth or water
2 tablespoons flour

Preheat oven to 350 degrees. In a shallow, wide bowl, crack eggs and then beat. In a separate bowl, combine breadcrumbs, paprika and Parmesan cheese. Thread pork and veal cubes onto skewers, alternating pork and veal pieces. Sprinkle threaded skewers with salt and pepper then dip meat in the egg then bread crumbs. Repeat on remaining skewers. Heat wide deep skillet and oil over medium-high heat to 350 degrees. Once hot, place skewers in the pan in batches. Reduce heat to medium, and brown on all sides, about 2-3 minutes per side. Once browned, transfer skewers to a baking dish and cover with foil. Bake, covered, for 20 minutes. While skewers bake, return to used skillet and add flour. Slowly whisk in stock, broth or water to liquefy flour and break up browned bits then let rest until meat is done cooking. Once meat is done cooking move skillet over medium heat and, while stirring constantly, bring to a boil. Simmer just until sauce thickens. Drizzle sauce over skewers and serve immediately. Yield: 4 servings. ~

A "sister from another mister" since 1979, Lori and I share a love of GOD, good family recipes, and all the great food we grew up on in the Calumet Region. Lori was kind enough to share her mom's favorite recipe for City Chicken.

A Calumet Region Rat, and a "sister from another mister" since 1986 (thanks to our work in the tool industry), Jen and I bonded instantly, making us both feel like we had known each other our whole lives. Perhaps because we share that Eastern European heritage, which makes us think and act alike sometimes-who knows!

A "sister from another mister" since 1986, Jen tells me that her adoring husband Arlen loves her from scratch cooking so much that he says things like, "We may not be spring chickens, but Jen's fresh-cooked pasta loaded with meatballs and sauce sure makes me feel like clucking!"

Jen and have remained friends ever since, despite both of us moving out of the Calumet Region. Her Eastern European ancestry and a love for cooking which, when coupled with growing up in the Calumet Region, always give us plenty of things to talk about as well as chew on.

Jen's Simply Superb Spaghetti Sauce

Yield: 6 servings

1 tablespoon good olive oil

1 sweet onion, minced

2-4 cloves garlic, minced

1/2 cup good red wine, or chicken broth

1 (28-ounce) can Pastorelli brand pizza sauce, or favorite sauce

1 tablespoon chopped fresh flat-leaf parsley

1 teaspoon unrefined sea salt

1 teaspoon freshly ground black pepper

Heat the olive oil in a large, 12-inch skillet. Add onion and sauté over medium heat until translucent, 5 to 10 minutes. Add garlic and cook for 1 minute more or until garlic starts to sing. Raise heat to high, add wine and cook, scraping up all the brown bits in the pan. Cook until almost all the liquid is gone, about 3 minutes. Stir in sauce, parsley, salt, and pepper. Cover, and simmer on the lowest heat for 15 minutes. Add cooked meatballs, if desired.

Jen's love of certain CR foods runs as deep as mine, so we now share stories about great meals that we used to have together there. Prompting us to joke every once in a while by saying, "Guess you can take the girl out of the Calumet Region, but you can never take the Calumet Region out of the girl!"

Married and living very happily on a farm in Indiana with her adorable husband, Arlen, Jen still loves to cook from scratch and make comfort meals for her husband. Here's one of his favorites that she's thrilled to share here with you!

Jen's Loaded Meatballs

Yield: 8 servings

2 eggs, lightly beaten
1 tablespoon Worcestershire sauce
2 large onions, finely chopped
2/3 cup plain or Italian bread crumbs
1/3 cup grated Parmesan cheese
1 tablespoon dried parsley
1 tablespoons dried basil
1 tablespoon dried oregano
8 garlic cloves, minced or pressed
1 teaspoon unrefined sea salt
1 teaspoon pepper
1/4 teaspoon cayenne powder (trust me)
1 pound ground beef or bison
1/2 pound ground pork
1/2 pound ground veal
16 fresh mini mozzarella cheese balls, drained and patted dry
Hot, cooked fresh spaghetti
Marinara or spaghetti sauce, warmed (see recipe)

In a large bowl, combine eggs, Worcestershire, onions, bread crumbs, Parmesan, parsley, basil, oregano, garlic, salt, peppers and meat.

Using a large fork, blend this mixture well then gently pull meat apart into small bits over mixture. Using a large fork, drag fork through bowl, gently flaking mixture upward until well blended. Do not use downward pressure or meat will toughen. Gently divide mixture into 16 portions then shape each portion around one of the mozzarella balls. Place meatballs in a shallow baking pan, and bake in a 400-degree, pre-heated oven for 20 minutes. While meatballs bake, make sauce, and cook spaghetti. ~

As my life extended outside of the Calumet Region, I was blessed to meet more "sisters from other misters," through the years, like Jenny, a Michigan native who I met back in 2008 through our shared love for cooking and generously sharing our favorite recipes whenever we can.

Jenny loves to give as well as receive the gift of food and she feels that any dish is a good dish to give.

"It's the act of giving – not what you are giving - that shows that you care, and the world would be a much nicer place if more people would think about that. To show people that they care about them, all the time."

Finding great comfort in her mother's recipes, Jenny said the one holiday recipe that will always remind her of her dear, departed mother is Hanky Pankys.

Jenny's Hanky Pankys

1 pound ground beef
1pound hot pork sausage
1 small onion, finely diced
16 ounces Velveeta cheese
Cayenne pepper
Red pepper flakes
1 loaf sliced rye cocktail bread

In a skillet, brown hamburger, sausage, and onion. Add Velveeta cheese until melted, sprinkle cayenne pepper and pepper flakes to taste.
Let cool completely.
Mound onto cocktail rye slices then bake at 350 degrees for 10-12 minutes or until bubbly.

Approximate servings per recipe: 10.

"Mom just loved "Hanky Pankys" so much!" Jenny said smiling, "and so did everyone else! They would just eat them up and there would never be any left!"

A fellow Hoosier native, from the far east side of the state, Debi has been a "sister from another mister" since 2008, when we met through work. A high-spirited friend who will drive a full two hours straight just to grab a slice at House of Pizza with us from the western side of her great state!

Debi does like to hang out with her friends, not her kitchen sink, as she says, so she prefers easy ways to whip up something wonderful and fast, like her E – Z Strawberry Pizza. "I'd much rather be out meeting new people and hanging with good friends and enjoying conversations" Debi said. "I don't like to be tied to the kitchen while everyone else is having fun, that's for sure!" she said with her girlish laugh. "I do like to bring a nice dish to gatherings because sharing food with friends and loved ones makes a gathering even more special in my book, and what girl doesn't want to make a dish that looks like you fussed all over it when in fact you didn't."

Debi's E-Z Strawberry Pizza

1 pkg. sugar cookie dough
8 ounces cream cheese
1 1/2 cups powdered sugar
1 teaspoon milk
1 teaspoon vanilla
1 package strawberry glaze
1 quart strawberries, sliced

Preheat oven to 350 degrees. Roll out cookie dough flat then place onto a parchment-lined or greased rimmed cookie sheet.

Bake for 10-12 minutes. Meanwhile, in a mixing bowl, combine cheese, sugar, milk and vanilla, beating until smooth.

Remove crust from oven and allow to cool before spreading cream cheese mixture across the top of baked cookie dough.

In a bowl, combine strawberries with strawberry glaze then spread on top of cheese sauce. Chill until serving.

Yield: 12 servings

"I think special times call for special looking food. I know it always makes me feel good when someone brings me a fabulous looking dish. Life doesn't get any sweeter than that, and you know how I like it sweet!"

Anne's Favorite Hungarian Mushroom Soup

6 tablespoons butter
1 1/2 cups chopped onion
4 teaspoons sweet Hungarian paprika
4 teaspoons dried dill weed
2 teaspoons salt
1 teaspoon black pepper
2/3 cup flour
1 2/3 cups milk
2 2/3 cups water
4 to 6 cups sliced white mushrooms*
3 tablespoons chopped fresh parsley
2 tablespoons soy sauce
2 tablespoons lemon juice
2/3 cup sour cream

In a Dutch oven or a deep skillet over medium heat, sauté onions in butter along with paprika, dill weed, salt and pepper. Whisk in flour then milk and water. Add mushrooms then bring almost to a boil. Reduce heat to a simmer, and let cook, uncovered, for 30 minutes.

Remove from heat. In a separate bowl, combine parsley, soy sauce, lemon juice and sour cream. Using a whisk, combine well then, while whisking, slowly pour some of the hot liquid from the soup into the sour cream mixture until the mixture begins to warm. Once sour cream mixture is no longer cold, stir into soup. Serve immediately. Yield: 2 to 3 quarts of soup.

NOTE: I usually double it because everyone likes it! Goes well with warm, crusty bread!

***= To clean mushrooms, use a clean damp cloth or dampened new sponge to remove all visible dirt/debris. It is best not to put them in water as they tend to absorb liquid and may not taste as good.**

"You know how much I enjoy the flavor of Eastern European food so I will have to share with you one of my favorite 'EE' soups!"

The universe has also blessed me with a "mother from another" in Anne in 2008, a dear friend and colleague who connects with me on so many different levels that it could fill a chapter by itself!Feeling like we have a mother-daughter connection void of any baggage, we've come to lovingly refer to each other in initials, "OM" for "Oregon Mom" and "MD" for "Michigan Daughter."

In addition to being an amazing word smith in her own right, Anne possesses "MacGyver" like talents that, like my cousin Elizabeth and sister Jeanne, include needles to do meticulous cross-stitch work, and a set of eagle eyes that enable her to catch all my dyslexic, south paw errors (when she's given the chance to review manuscripts before they go to print).

GOD knew exactly what HE was doing when HE put the two of us in each other's lives. Though meeting in Michigan, Anne did reside briefly in the Calumet Region, and was thrilled to help me with this Midwest-minded project.

To me the biggest "WIN" that comes out of my kitchen is when I see it bring happiness to others. When my wonderful husband, Richard, shoots me a compliment about a dish, it reminds me of how Dad used to compliment Mom, touching my heart in ways no trophy ever could.

Sharing the common bond of being raised in the Whiting-Robertsdale area of the Calumet Region (but not crossing paths until we both moved away), we didn't realize just how much we were rooted to our hometown until we began to reminisce and agree with the old cliche, "You can take the person out of the Calumet Region, but you can never take the Calumet Region out of the person!"

We also discovered that our fathers knew each other, worked at the same place, and that my husband had inherited some items from his father that my own dad had made. I was stunned!

My Calumet Region husband is a man who never seems to sit still. He loves to work with his hands, which helps to display that he also possesses some awesome "MacGyver" skills.

Loving to fiddle over a fire, whether its to cook up fish or cook down sap, it's hard not to love a guy who will painstakingly trudge through knee-deep snow to collect sap and boil it down into a marvelous maple syrup that shimmers gold, just so I can enjoy cooking with it and add its delightful flavor to meals we make at home.

Not afraid to don an apron at will or pick up a rolling pin, it's not unusual to find Richard playing with some roskie dough once the holidays start marching in.

Implementing his own kaizen into the mix, Richard finds that placing the filling in zipper bags (then snipping one corner away) is the most clean and efficient way to pipe those fillings in. I thank God for Richard every day because life couldn't be any better than it is.

The Calumet Region has blessed my life in many ways, most especially when it brought a fellow native into mine. It also gave me a brother-in-law, George, and two sisters-in-law, Maryann and Judy, that I now get to call "kin."

Richard also helped me to discover a new (old) love, which entails going off-grid.

Offering authentic granite surfaces on which to cook
and water that's clean enough to drink
the Boundary Waters offer a much-needed respite
clearing the mind and spirit, enabling you to fully breathe.

Reminding me of those days in childhood
when we'd cook those old cans of string beans
our trips into the Boundary Waters bring about
a full-circle moment for me.

Revealing that perhaps what is most important to see
is that the best things in life are indeed
always free!

Arriving right back where I began
cooking over an open fire along a water's edge
I find that I am my happiest
when in close communion with Nature
and my life is in
God's hands.

Richard Taylor enjoying the Boundary Waters at Quetico Provincial Park, Ontario Canada
Text and photo by Laura Kurella

IV

BONUS: Winners, Wieners + Secrets

My interest in food has clearly evolved throughout my life and has been further influenced by all aspects of my life. Formed initially around the recipes from the "old country," these oh-so-comforting dishes provided the perfect foundation for me to infuse my mini "MacGyver" to build an interesting recipe collection.

Spending my first forty years living predominantly in the Calumet Region, I wasn't inspired to re-create any Calumet Region dishes until I migrated to Michigan, which made me miss them.

With changes in life and location providing me exposure to the richness of what the Great Lakes Region has to offer us, both my palate and my recipe binder grew as inspirations came floating in! I can still recall my first Michigan produce "crush" because it is still a love that you will always find somewhere in my kitchen, and that is Michigan berries! Their taste, wide availability, and great, fresh farm stand prices lured me like a moth to the flame and got me to experiment with them continually.

The same is true for short-seasoned Michigan asparagus, all the fabulous summer fruits and fresh fall produce, too. It's almost never-ending, even in northern Michigan, especially if you take care to squirrel away items for winter use.

This winter we're playing with garden-grown organic Italian kale. Dehydrating whole leaves then de-veining and vacuum storing as both flakes and powder form. I figure it's more economical to store it this way, offer convenience, and new ways to sneak it into food!

Having such an abundance of delightful Michigan farm-fresh produce severely altered the way I cook, causing the ingredient to become the catalyst, not the recipe, and making me shop in reverse! I no longer headed to the market with a recipe in hand. Instead, I went with an open mind and open hand, looking for the best there was.

Making this switch, using an ingredient and not a recipe as my muse, caused a shift in my cooking paradigm that, in a larger sense, made me feel like a kid on the day their training wheels came off!

Inspired by Michigan produce and equally fascinated by the process of developing new recipes and the joy they brought to others created a new, synergistic energy that nudged into daring to dip my spatula into the world of food sport challenges. It just needed to find a little nerve (and courage) is all. God bless Michigan produce!

The act of developing an original recipe in the hopes of it becoming award-winning is both a challenge and a reward. While I cannot say with any certainty how many contests I have entered, I can say that I have lost far more than I've won. Either way, I do end up with a prize because the act of challenging myself awards me with sharper cooking skills and a little tougher skin. Then on rare occasions I get the wonderful news of a recipe win!

When I first started entering recipe contests, I took a run at just about anything that I was qualified to enter, which was tricky because there are contests exclusively for chefs, which I am not, and there are contests that are exclusive to amateur home cooks, which I may not be qualified to enter. This is because I have received compensation for demonstrating/teaching cooking, and do get paid to write about food and recipes which, in some circles elevates me to that of a food profes-sional. Given all that, I exist in a precarious position that places me somewhere between an amateur home cook and a professional chef, which enables me to only enter contests that are open to anyone of any kind, thus reducing this gal's food sport opportunities exponentially.

For me, stepping up to a food challenge is akin to solving a puzzle, and anyone who likes jigsaws knows what satisfaction comes from popping in that last piece. That's exactly how it feels when I create a new recipe, which is then magnified (ten-fold) if the recipe manages to ascend to award-winning.

One contest that got my creative juices flowing (spoiler alert: I didn't win) called for you to demonstrate a creative way to draw the public's interest in a brand of hot sauce. Each month there was a specific challenge, and while I don't recall the contest specifics, I do remember the fun I had creating my entries.
Going to great lengths, I even bought scale props to make my food scenes more life-like.

In one I created a miniature tailgate scene that was just too cute. I thought it was unforgettable, but unfortunately, got beat out by a woman who got a sleeve tattoo featuring a bottle of the brand's hot sauce. Apparently, marking yourself for life was more appealing to the brand than my cute "Hot" dog action scene!

I will never forget the thrill of winning my first national contest though, which came during a very dizzying year because it was rife with many changes in both my personal and professional life. The win was also the very first one to qualify for a spot in the World Food Championships (WFC), my first global competition (in the Seafood category). I earned it through winning the qualifier competition that Penobscot & McCrum, a Maine-based potato company, sponsored.

Naturally, all entries needed to elevate potatoes to a new level, so I put my thinking cap on which, for some reason, made me think of nothing but lobster. Perhaps because the contest sponsor was located in Maine. I decided to lean into it and, thanks be to God, it won!

Basing my recipe on how I don't like having to "fish" for lobster in bowls of bisque, I decided to turn lobster bisque on its tail, and I do mean that literally, by serving a little bisque with that lobster instead! I elevated my recipe even further by giving a special nod to the event sponsor by serving my soup inside a deliciously-crisp and toasty-warm potato boat that Penobscot & McCrum just happens to sell frozen and ready for use!
FYI: This recipe can be served with or without the potato boats as my photo demonstrates.

Running my Bodacious Lobster Bisque entry to the judges at the 2015 World Food Championships.
This was my first time competing at a global level. Boy was I nervous!
Courtesy of World Food Championships

My prize-winning Bodacious "Bathing Beauty" Lobster Bisque turns this traditional soup on its tail, literally, which ensures you won't need to "fish" for lobster in your bisque anymore!

Bodacious "Bathing Beauty" Lobster Bisque

Yield: 6 servings.

3 tablespoons butter
3 tablespoons virgin olive oil
2 tablespoons chopped onion
2 tablespoons chopped celery
2 tablespoons chopped carrot
1/4 cup chopped fresh mushrooms
15 ounces chicken broth
1/8 teaspoon salt
1/8 teaspoon cayenne pepper
1 1/2 cups half-and-half
1/2 cup dry white wine
1-pound small, raw lobster tails, rinsed, de-veined split lengthwise
6 - 8 Penobscot McCrum Baked Skins Boats

In a large skillet over medium-high heat, combine butter, olive oil, onion, celery, and carrot. Cook and stir until onions begin to caramelize - about 15 minutes. Add mushrooms and cook until they soften slightly. Add chicken broth and cayenne pepper. Bring to a boil then simmer for 20 minutes. Prepare potato boats by baking, broiling, or frying until crispy, then hold warm. Pour broth mixture into a blender (or an emulsion blender) and process until very smooth. Return to heat, stir in the half-and-half and white wine. Bring to a simmer then add prepped lobster tails. Reduce heat to low and cook over low heat for about 30 minutes. Remove tails and shred or chop all but 6 of the halves into the soup, discarding the shell. Serve by placing one-half of a lobster tail (shell on or off) in a potato boat then drench in bisque. ~

Prize-winning version of my recipe featured toasted crisp potato boats

A recipe entry representing the State of Michigan, and our love for fresh produce and hearty-meaty sandwiches, my Tempting Teres Tenderloin Tower, won a "Top 10" award in the "Taste of America" contest, which also awarded me a second chance to compete at the 2021 WFC, in the Sandwich category. I was extremely honored that this recipe won, but due to an important and long-standing prior commitment, which involved an entire community, I was not able to attend WFC that year.

Mouth-watering amazing, my prize-winning Tempting Teres Tenderloin Tower is one sandwich that needs no bread!

Tempting Teres Tenderloin Tower

Yield: 2 servings

2 (8-ounce) Teres Major Tenderloin* fillets, 1 1/2 inches thick

SAUCE

1 head roasted garlic

1/2 tablespoon butter

1/2 tablespoon olive oil

RUB

1 tablespoon olive oil

1 teaspoon kosher salt

1/2 teaspoon pepper, coarsely ground

SKILLET DRIPPINGS

1 tablespoon olive oil

2 tablespoons butter

1 teaspoon Worcestershire sauce

2 tablespoons dry sherry

1/2 teaspoon your favorite sweetener

To begin, squeeze each head of roasted garlic to expel the cloves into a bowl, add 1/2 tablespoon of melted butter and 1/2 tablespoon of olive oil to the garlic, stir together and set aside, reserving 2 tablespoons. Preheat the grill to 400 degrees. Rub steaks with 1 tablespoon olive oil then liberally season with salt and pepper and set aside. Place steaks on a preheated grill and sear well for 1 minute on each side, turning halfway through to create grill marks. Move steaks to a cast iron skillet or other heatproof grill pan, then pour all but 2 tablespoons of the garlic-infused oil/butter sauce over steaks. Place the pan on indirect heat of the grill and close the grill cover. Cook for 7 minutes for medium rare. Remove the steaks from the pan to a warm plate and cover with foil. Let rest for 5 to 8 minutes. Meanwhile, in the same skillet, add sherry, sweetener, beef broth, Worcestershire, and remaining 2 tablespoons garlic-infused oil/butter. Cook over high heat, blending well, until it boils then reduce to a simmer and cook until reduced by half. To plate, lay a bed of greens down on a plate then drizzle with skillet sauce. In the center of the plate, place a fresh slice of tomato drizzled with sauce, then top with a fresh slice of red onion and drizzle with more sauce. Top with a piece of Teres Tenderloin then drizzle with more sauce. Repeat the assembly method two more times to create a tower that features a trifecta of flavor. Finish plate with a sprinkling of Feta or Bleu cheese crumbles, and serve extra sauce alongside.

*=Any tenderloin will do. ~

One of my proudest wins came when one of my recipes won a "Most Innovative" award in the Taste of Home Magazine's "Recipes Across America" contest. Made to represent the great State of Michigan, I named it, "Michigan Cherry 'Zing' Japanese-style Cheesecake," after Michigan's incredible tart Montmorency cherry crop.

My prize-winning, Michigan Cherry Japanese-style Cheesecake offers the delightful aroma, taste, and beauty of Michigan's most beloved Montmorency cherry, which serves as the crowning touch on this marvelous angel food-meets-New York cheesecake dessert...Oh my!

Michigan Cherry "Zing" Japanese-style Cheesecake

4 ounces Neufchatel (or cream) cheese, room temp
7 tablespoons butter, room temp, divided use
2/3 cup heavy cream
12 eggs
1 1/4 cups sugar, divided use
2 teaspoons pure vanilla extract
1 lemon (zest only)
1/4 cup all-purpose flour
5 tablespoons cornstarch, divided use
2 cups tart Michigan Cherries (fresh or frozen)
1/4 teaspoon cayenne powder (the "Zing), optional)
1/2 cup cold water

Preheat the oven to 325 degrees. Place a large brownie or lasagna size pan in the oven and then fill to a 1/2-inch depth of water. Line the sides of a 9-inch spring-form pan with a 4-inch collar of parchment paper then cut a circle to fit the bottom of the pan, overlapping sides slightly, then set aside.

In a small saucepan over medium heat, whisk cream cheese and 6 tablespoons butter until smooth. Remove from heat and whisk in cream until smooth then set aside to let cool. Separate eggs, reserving 6 yolks for another purpose.

In the bowl of a stand mixer fitted with a whisk, beat 12 egg whites until you see soft peaks. Slowly add 3/4 cup sugar while continuing to beat until shiny peaks form. While whites beat, in a separate large bowl, using a hand whisk, whisk 6 egg yolks until smooth, then slowly drizzle in cooled down cream cheese mixture, stirring until evenly combined. Whisk in vanilla and lemon zest just to combine then, in a sifter utensil, combine flour and 4 tablespoons of the cornstarch then sift into cheese mixture making sure to avoid any lumps. Once egg whites form shiny peaks, fold one third of the whites into the cheese mixture, then fold in remaining whites until thoroughly combined. Pour batter into prepared spring-form pan then carefully lower cake into the water-filled pan that's been preheating in oven. Bake for 25 minutes, then reduce heat to 280 degrees. Bake for an additional 55 minutes, or until the cake has risen to almost double its height and center cracks. (Crack will disappear as cake cools) While cake bakes, make topping.

Wash, stem, and pit cherries, if needed. In a medium saucepan, combine remaining tablespoon of butter, remaining 1/2 cup sugar, remaining tablespoon cornstarch, cayenne, and water.

Over medium heat, stir until cornstarch liquefies and mixture begins to boil. Reduce heat to a simmer, then cook while stirring, until thickened and slightly reduced, about five minutes.

Set aside and allow to cool completely.

When cake is finished baking, remove pan from water bath and set on stove. Loosen rim from pan with a knife; remove foil. Remove the rim from pan; remove paper.

Serve cheesecake warm, sprinkled with powdered sugar then topped with prepared cherry topping. Store cake and topping in refrigerator. Yield: 8 servings ~

My Crunchy Roasted Garlic Florentine Artichoke Flutes with Oniony-Garlic Butter Sauce won a 1st Place Prize in the 2022 Heinz 57 Culinary Collection Sauce recipe contest. This sauce is good you'll be tempted to eat it straight from the jar! It reminds me of the bread-dipping sauce served in upscale Italian restaurants. So good!

Crunchy Roasted Garlic Florentine Artichoke Flutes & Garlic Butter Sauce

Yield: Approximately 15 flutes (8 servings)

1 jar Heinz 57 Roasted Garlic Culinary Crunch Sauce, divided use
4 ounces cream cheese, at room temperature
4 ounces shredded Monterey Jack cheese
1/2 cup freshly-grated Parmesan
1/4 cup mayonnaise
1 tablespoon fresh minced rosemary (or 1/2 tablespoon dried)
1/2 teaspoon sea salt
1/2 teaspoon black pepper
3 tablespoons fresh-snipped chives (optional)
10-ounces frozen leaf spinach, thawed, drained well
14-ounces canned small artichoke hearts, drained well
1 pkg egg roll wrappers
Oil, for cooking (or nonstick cooking spray for alternate cooking method)
1/3 cup of melted butter
1/4 cup extra virgin olive oil

Stir the jar of Roasted Garlic Culinary Crunch well then measure out 1/4 cup and place in the bowl of a food processor. Add cream cheese, Monterey Jack (or provolone), Parmesan, mayonnaise, rosemary, salt, pepper, and chives (if using). Process until smooth and well blended, then stop the processor. Using your hands or the back of a spoon, squeeze/press all the liquid from spinach, getting it as dry as possible, then add it to the processor bowl, and process until blended well. Drain artichoke hearts well, then chop coarsely by hand, or add artichokes to the processor bowl and pulse them for a finer dice, if desired. Line a pan (that will fit into your freezer) with plastic wrap, parchment, or wax paper and set aside. Move filling to a bowl and add artichokes, if chopped by hand and stir together. Place about 3 tablespoons of filling on the center of an egg roll wrapper. Spread filling out to a strip 1 inch wide by 5 inches long, then wet edges of dough with water and roll up according to egg roll wrapper package instructions. Place filled flute onto the prepared pan and repeat with remaining wrappers. Place pan of filled flutes into the freezer to rest/set up. To prepare Dipping Sauce: In a small bowl, using a small whisk, combine remaining Roasted Garlic Culinary Crunch Sauce with the melted butter and olive oil. Whisk until well blended then set aside in a warm spot.

To Fry Flutes: In a Dutch oven (to prevent spatter) bring 1 to 2 inches of your preferred oil to 360 degrees. Carefully lower the flutes into hot oil and cook, turning, until they puff up a bit and brown nicely, about 6 to 8 minutes. Drain on a wire rack, or drain cloth/paper, for 3 minutes before serving.

To Air Fry or Bake: Preheat the oven to 400 degrees. Spray rolls (on all sides) with cooking spray then bake, turning halfway through cooking time, until slightly puffed and nicely browned on all sides, about 10 to 15 minutes. Slice rolls in half, on a diagonal, if desired, and serve with Garlic Butter Sauce.~

A huge "Thank you!" to everyone who supported this recipe by voting for it because thanks to you, it won the 2022 "People's Choice" award in the Minnesota Cultivated Wild Rice "Get WILD with Wild Rice" recipe contest!

Made by using a special "popping" method, which elevates the rice's flavor to a nutty crunchy wonderful, the folks at Minnesota Rice liked it enough to also award it the coveted, "GOLDEN TICKET" to compete at the 2022 World Food Championships!

I am honored and thrilled because I was hoping to bring attention to this "popping" method in a big way because I found it enables you to prepare wild rice more quickly, and more flavorful, too!

KEYS TO "POPPING" SUCCESS!

1. Rice needs to be dry, whether cooked or uncooked
2. Oil needs to be about 365 degrees, whether deep-fried or pan-fried.

COOKED RICE VERSUS UNCOOKED RICE

Cooked (and dried) rice renders a light, crispy, crunchy, popped grain goodness. Uncooked, dry rice imparts a nuttier, toothy crunch and taste.

NOTE: Once popped, both cooked and uncooked rice can be quickly re-hydrated in any hot liquid (in equal parts), rendering them both into tender grains quite like boiled.

HOW TO POP (Uncooked) Minnesota "Popped" Cultivated Raw Wild Rice

A great way to infuse both convenience and creativity in your menu planning, while elevating the flavor of Minnesota's finest to a whole new flavor experience! Uncooked rice imparts a more toothy, nutty crunch and taste in every pop. Plus, you can hydrate into nutty tender rice by simply simmering it in your favorite liquid (equal parts) for a few minutes.

2 tablespoons favorite oil/fat

1/2 cup (uncooked) Minnesota Cultivated Wild Rice

Sea salt, to taste

In a heavy-bottomed medium saucepan with a tight-fitting lid over medium-high heat, add oil and monitor with an instant read thermometer, waiting for pan to reach 365 degrees.

When pot reaches temperature, add the rice, then swirl pan to coat the rice with the hot oil.

Cover the pan, reduce the heat to medium-high, remove lid and start stirring.

Once you don't hear any more popping, after about 7 minutes, turn off the heat, remove from the stove, and sprinkle with salt, or to taste.

Serve warm when possible. ~

Earning multple prizes, these Minnesota "Popped" Espresso Mocha Pillow Pops are as fun to make as they are to eat and the espresso can be swapped out with cocoa or cinnamon or anything that you like!

Minnesota "Popped" Espresso Mocha Pillow Crisps

Yield: 6 servings

1 cup cooked then dried Minnesota Cultivated Wild Rice*
1-inch favorite cooking oil
1 teaspoon espresso powder
1 pinch of Vietnamese cinnamon
1 cup semi-sweet mini chocolate chips
1/2 teaspoon vegetable shortening
1/2 teaspoon natural sea salt
12 regular marshmallows, cut in half to form 2 narrow circles
24 long toothpicks (or similar)

Line a rimmed baking sheet with a few layers of clean newspaper or paper bags covered by a layer of paper towel, or just paper towels, then set aside.

In a deep 2-quart saucepan fitted with an instant read thermometer (or a thermostat-controlled electric skillet), heat oil over medium-high heat until it reaches 365 degrees. Test oil for readiness by dropping a couple of dry rice grains into the hot oil. Rice will pop, puff and float to surface when oil is ready.

Using a small mesh strainer that is able to be lowered into the hot oil, pour one quarter of the dried rice into the strainer then lower the strainer into the hot oil. The rice will begin to pop after about 10 to 20 seconds of being in the oil. As popped rice floats to the top of the oil, use strainer to lift the popped grains out of the oil and transfer to a paper towel-lined rimmed baking sheet.

Repeat process with remaining rice, then remove pan of oil from heat and set aside.

Place the warm, popped rice in a medium bowl then sprinkle it with the cinnamon and espresso powder, tossing to blend in well, then set aside.

In a glass 2-cup measure or similar, combine chocolate chips, shortening, and salt then microwave in 15 to 30 second increments, stirring in-between, until melted. Line a serving dish with parchment or wax paper and set next to workstation. Thread one marshmallow onto a toothpick then dip into the melted chocolate, then press all sides into the spiced popped rice grains, and set down on paper-lined dish. Repeat with remaining marshmallows. Place dish in refrigerator until serving.

*= Contest required that you use conventionally cooked rice as an ingredient.

It was a happy accident in my kitchen that led me to discover how to pop wild rice. When I found it not only elevated the flavor of the wild rice in a way that makes it taste incredibly nutty, crunchy, and earthy, but also converts it into a quick-cooking rice, I got super excited!

I am so glad that it won so that more people will become aware of the awesome technique I uncovered, and will take a chance by trying wild rice in this form because it makes it so much more flavorful, faster to prepare, and so much more fun to eat. Get "Popping!"

I find the flavor of popped wild rice addicting. Its amazing aroma, nutty flavor, and oh-so-delightful crunch is just awesome, even alone as a snack.

Like a catalyst, it inspired me to create Snap, Crackle, 'Popped' Poppers, 'Popped' Wild Rice Ice Cream Pops, and Nutty-Crunchy 'Popped' Cran Slaw. While none of these recipes won, they did all tasted like winners to us! Perhaps proving in the end that it doesn't matter if your recipes are winners or wieners, just that they make you (and your family) feel good!

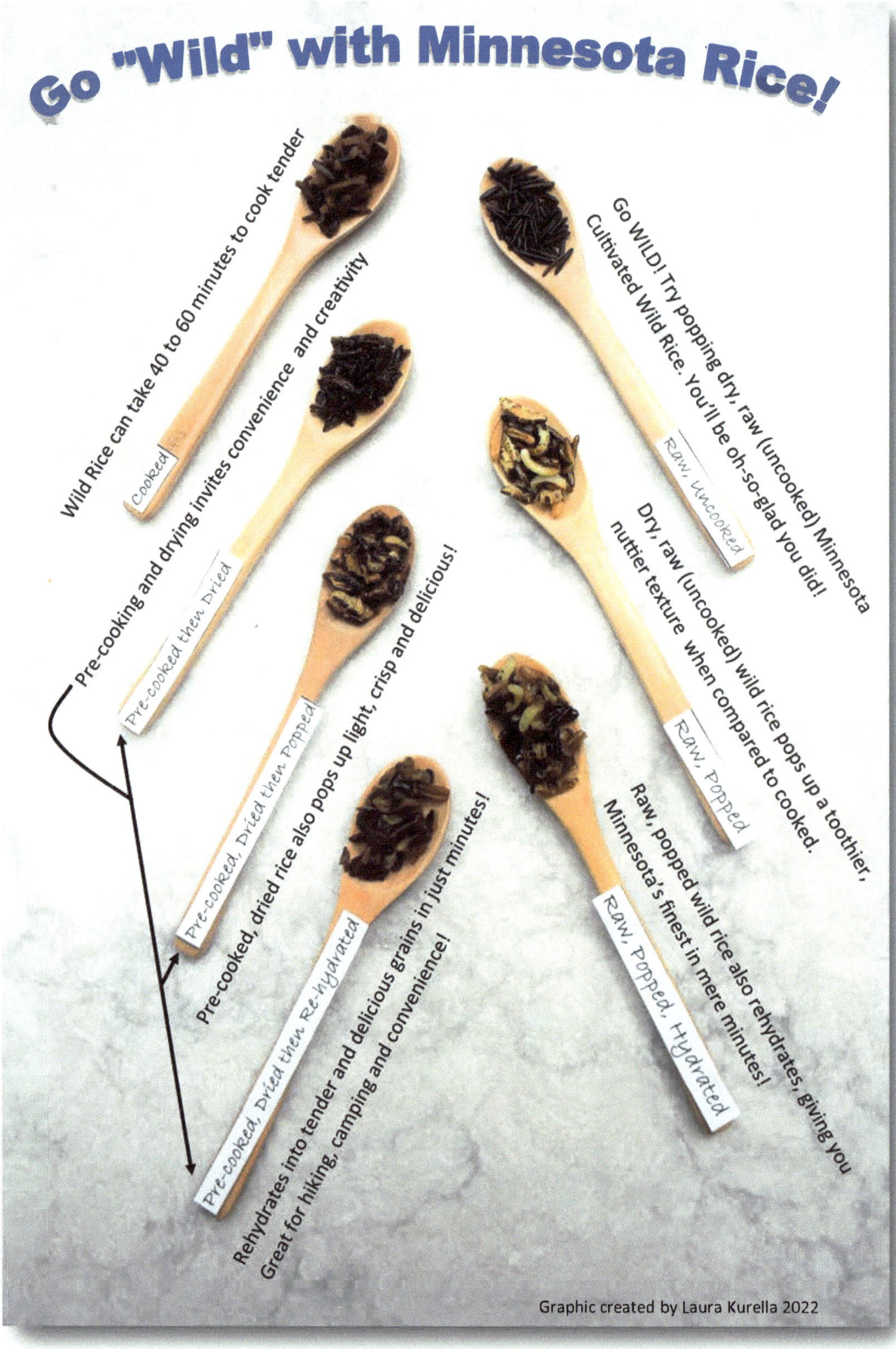
Go "Wild" with Minnesota Rice!
Wild Rice can take 40 to 60 minutes to cook tender
Cooked
Pre-cooking and drying invites convenience and creativity
Pre-cooked then Dried
Pre-cooked, dried rice also pops up light, crisp and delicious!
Pre-cooked, Dried then Popped
Rehydrates into tender and delicious grains in just minutes!
Great for hiking, camping and convenience!
Pre-cooked, Dried then Re-hydrated
Go WILD! Try popping dry, raw (uncooked) Minnesota
Cultivated Wild Rice. You'll be oh-so-glad you did!
Raw, Uncooked
Dry, raw (uncooked) wild rice pops up a toothier,
nuttier texture when compared to cooked.
Raw, Popped
Raw, popped wild rice also rehydrates, giving you
Minnesota's finest in mere minutes!
Raw, Popped, Hydrated
Graphic created by Laura Kurella 2022

The most frequently asked question (FAQ) I get about entering recipe contests is "What's your secret?" My top answer (tip) is to start by looking to see what has won the contest in the past (if it is an annual event) because this appears to be the greatest predictor of what their judges are drawn to. For example, if you see that year after year, they seem to choose an eye-appealing traditional soup over an original signature dish, then it's not worth racking your brain to develop something new when an eye-appealing soup is what will give you the leg up on the competition.

Another excellent tip came to me from the WFC Pasta Queen, Suzanne Clark. She conveyed that the most important thing a contestant needs to do is remember the key ingredient needs to be the "star" in the recipe, not a side show. Considering that this gal has won some big cooking competitions, it's safe to say that her advice is well worth taking. God bless Suzanne for being so kind to share one of her amazing tips to help get your recipe into the winner's circle!

An essential tip, because many recipes get tossed out before being considered because of poor writing, is to make sure you write clear and concise instructions. A big part of entering any recipe competition is following the general guidelines for recipe writing, which have changed. Short-hand is no longer accepted. A tablespoon needs to be written out as such in lowercase. A capital "T" is not acceptable, nor is Tbsp.

Ingredients are not capitalized unless you mention a name, and you need to be very specific in the instructions, and mention dimensions, such as 8 x 8 x 2-inch metal or glass brownie pan.

Ingredients should always be listed in order of use and include specifics such as, 1 carrot, chopped or 1 cup chopped carrots, for example.

My most important step with recipe entries is testing it out on others, both the written version and the actual food. The more people you have taste it the better too, because they will give you honest feedback that can help you tinker with it to make it taste better, too!

RULES TO RECIPE ENTRY WRITING *(unless otherwise instructed)*

1. No abbreviations
2. Don't capitalize unless it's a name
3. Always list the ingredients in the order of use
4. Always note if an ingredient has divided use
5. Instructions should list vessel, then method, then ingredient. "In a bowl, using a hand whisk (or fork), beat eggs and milk together well."
6. Always print out your entry and prepare it using the print out to help you find errors and make changes before you turn it in.
7. Give samples out to get opinions on appearance, taste and suggestions.

I have lots of guinea pigs, so perhaps that is my biggest my winning secret!

Good luck and remember to tap into that inner "MacGyver" in you!

Enjoy!

ABOUT THE AUTHOR

| 147 |

148

About the Author

Born and raised in the Calumet region of northwest Indiana, an area so close to the Loop that it's considered a Chicago suburb, Laura credits this "melting pot" with having had a great influence on her palate.

Affected by the tragic death of their father, which came as the result of clogged arteries, taking him at age 58, Laura put herself on a mission to find food that is more helpful and less harmful to the body.
Spending the past twenty years chronicling this journey in what has become an award-winning, syndicated newspaper food column written under her name, Laura remains tireless in her pursuit of "Food that makes you feel good!"

Using her free time to help sharpen her self-taught cooking skills, Laura's foray into the world of recipe contests has helped her to evolve into an award-winning recipe developer at a national level.
Midwest Morsels is her third cookbook in print, and the first she has designed, created, and self-published, which she chose to do to control content, design, costs, and distribution.

Laura has also authored the children's book, "A Delicious Day at Mrs. K's," which is named in honor of their mom, and turns her own grandchildren into the colorful characters in this book that teaches pre-K through second graders the importance of nutrition and why it is so vital to seek it first. Laura's hope is that by arming our little ones with this crucial knowledge we can help them to develop into healthier adults that pass on this crucial key to better health and vitality to future generations.

About the Editor

Born in Indiana, raised in Michigan, and currently residing in Oregon, Anne Sutton attributes her love of words to her father's avid interest in lexicology. "I recall a game my father and I used to play," she mused. "I would look up long words in the dictionary, say them, and then he would define them through his knowledge of the Latin and Greek languages, even if he had never heard the word before!"

Retiring in 1995, Sutton spent the next 20 years volunteering for the American Red Cross and various other organizations, as well as two church offices, which is how/where she and Laura Kurella first crossed paths.

Forming a bond similar to that of mother and daughter (only better), their shared love of God, The Word, the written word, and recipes stirred up a conversation between them that has been unbroken since 2008.
Lending her natural, God-given editing skills to help repair Laura's dizzying dyslexic issues,

Anne has been at the helm to edit two of Laura's previous cookbooks and her children's book, which teaches little ones the importance of nutrition and the need to seek it first. "Truly, the universe knew what it was doing when it put the two of us together!" Kurella sighed.

CPSIA information can be obtained
at www.ICGtesting.com
Printed in the USA
BVHW012325011222
653249BV00001B/9

* 9 7 8 0 9 7 6 6 3 0 3 9 5 *